New poetry   I

An anthology edited by
Peter Porter and Charles Osborne

The Arts Council of Great Britain

New Poetry 1 published 1975
© 1975, The Arts Council of Great Britain

The copyright of each poem remains with the poet

Published by The Arts Council of Great Britain
105 Piccadilly, London W1V 0AU

Hardback: ISBN 0 7287 0052 2
Paperback: ISBN 0 7287 0053 0

Designed and printed in England
by Shenval Press, London and Harlow

CONTENTS

In this, the first of the Arts Council's yearly anthologies of contemporary British poetry, the editors were presented with an extremely simple set of premises but an extremely wide-ranging body of work to choose from. The catchment area for the anthology (and the same will be true of its successors) was the period immediate to the closing date of entries – which in this case was the end of May 1974. The only stipulations were that no poem should have been published in book form at the time of submission and that the poet should be a British subject, though not necessarily resident in the United Kingdom. Each poet was invited to submit six poems, but no restriction was placed upon their length. Thus, the arena was open to anybody who wrote poetry – from the most celebrated poet in the land to the previously unpublished aspirant. The Editors were conscious of their responsibility in suppressing their own partialities to styles and allegiances. This does not mean that they were naive or ignorant, but that, in assessing the merits of each person's work, they were careful to judge whether it was good of its kind – not whether they liked that kind. Not being nonpareils, they may have misjudged some contributions, but they are delighted to be able to offer a far wider and more catholic range of work than is usually to be found in such anthologies. In this they were helped by what would otherwise have seemed an almost intoler-able burden – the sheer weight of work submitted. They had to find the time to read more than 42,000 poems. At the end, they found they had compiled a rich and remarkable body of poetry – something, in fact, to oppose the voices of doom which are constantly being raised against the fallen state of British poetry. Judged by the historical imperatives of Modernism or by the self-inflating canons of fashion, an anthology like this will seem to lack direction. It is not prescriptive, nor was it put together by market-survey methods. It may or may not be representative, but it is undoubtedly full of worthwhile poems.

At the moment, there is no similar anthology being produced in these islands. The annual PEN anthology now restricts itself to work which has appeared in magazines, and it does not solicit contributions. *Poetry Dimension* is selected from magazines, books and other printed sources. Most occasional anthologies have particular loyalties to subject, place or some set of critical or aesthetic propositions. There are also the many Vanity Press annuals, which publish virtually anything, however bad, but which insist on the contributors paying to have their work included. The Arts Council not only imposes no fee on submission, it also pays for every poem printed and at a generous rate. But these facts are recorded merely to establish the fairness used in producing a state-subsidised anthology. The point of the book is the work to which it gives an outlet. The editors were delighted to come upon many names which they did not know and to be able to print much which is original and unprecedented. It was, perhaps, disappointing not to receive contributions from many of the best-known poets now writing in Britain, but the temptation to approach some of them in order to stiffen the contents page with famous reputations was strongly resisted. The Editors' brief for the anthology was the straightforward one of helping poets to have their work read by a wider public. It is to be hoped that the contents of these pages put the recurring factionalism of the British literary world into perspective: most poets are their own men and less than comfortable in the uniforms which critics give them.

Peter Porter
Charles Osborne

New poetry

The Virgin of Mileševa

The centuries flow over the Church at Mileševa
And the frescoes have withdrawn a little in time –
Only so much as makes dust of dark in the sky
When the night comes, bringing stars.
They are inaccessible
Except to the utmost quiet of receiving;
Withdrawn from a world of noise they are always there,
Saying, the waves reached this point, there are mountains so high;
We know where we are.
The Virgin is still, in her quaintly jewelled chair.
The little Church behind her has rounded windows
With six panes: its roof is blue like her folded dress;
A cloudy blue, with dark shadows.
In her left hand is a pink flower;
Her face is beautiful with meditation
And the halo is old and sombre gold.
A spear of light has touched her – divine illumination?
Or is it the spear that would pierce her heart also?
All is still and attained:
From this moment all is accomplished.
Already the Angel points to the tomb: it is empty.
Not a flower lost, no fold of the Virgin's dress.
How can we touch them?
They are untouchable.
Time falls, but it is not time that is between us;
Time has preserved this perfection, this virginity.
The centuries fall like dusk over Mileševa,
As if it were not time but eternity that is falling.

I
Mary-Mary, I'm no longer afraid of
sundays.   The lidded streets.   The

scribbling on the walls
children-high.   They never say

  – oh Jesus, it's monday!   So you
should understand my chronicle

of everyday weariness.   You who
loved being pregnant,   curving your hands

  – all out to here, she says.   Endlessly
plotting how the foetus lay.

      Flowers for
a love, she staggered at the kerb, clasping
carnations. O, my boozey love, the sad
eyeballs. Candles and even
soft Delius, hurt

the dark one's head.
(she hurts my heart! I
find people lucky if they've
got a lover to hate) Gas bills
and parts for the cooker

clamoured and made exasperate
the life of Mary-Mary. (*she became
hard, belovèd, my love
these overworked*

words she is shy of)

She thinks we tell
secrets with more than our mouths.

Each morning from its corner loomed
the smug-leggèd desk. The drawers
bosoming, it boomed out – come now,
come over here and do your bit. It

would not take Mary-mary to rest. With full
matronly misunderstanding it enquired
how the work was going – can I offer
you a felt-tip? do you need perhaps

a staple or a dog-clip? The typewriter,
old faithful that once she loved, lay
morose with dust. Both of them calling
her the cuckoo, in this her own nest. She

swore at them, depressed. You've had your whack!
Take away my wig and my teeth, said she,
and I'll sit up in bed like an egg
and by God, I'll crack.

Totes Meer – by Paul Nash. 1940–41

1

This picture is of waste. No victory
gloats in the absent eye that we make ours
by seeing what it saw. But tragedy
is not stressed either – we may keep our tears.

No beggar whimpers for them, we are shown
no scars, no mutilations, no burnt boys
but, bleached by moonlight, aircraft wreckage thrown
into an open grave for broken toys.

An Icarus has fallen from the sky.
Another and another fall, a rain
of torches must have fallen. This clear eye
records the waste, does not insist on pain.

Pity withheld is power; a reservoir
of weeping gathers, war-dammed in the brain.

2

The time is dawn. The moon
hangs on withdrawing dark
shedding just light enough
to cast shadows that mark
the sand. On ragged waves –
as rigid in arrest
as signpost dead – each crest
postures as though it lives,
threatens but cannot reach
with more than shadow-claws
the dead sea's desert beach:
yet this dry tide still gnaws
the fields away; lost land
submerges, all but drowned,

In the Terai

Our throats full of dust, teeth harsh with it,
plastery sweat in our hair and nostrils,
we slam the flaps of the Landrover down
and think we choke on these roads.
Well, they will be better in time:
all along the dry riverbed
just as when we drove past this morning
men and women squatting under umbrellas
or cloth stretched over sticks, or nothing,
are splitting chipped stones to make smaller chips,
picking the fingernail-sized fragments
into graded heaps: roads by the handful.
We stop at the village and buy glasses of tea,
stewed and sweet; swallow dust with it
and are glad enough. The sun tilts lower.
Somewhere, surely, in its valley
under cool thatch mothers are feeding children
with steamy rice, leaning over them
to pour milk or water; the cups
tasting of earthenware, neutral, clean,
the young heads smelling only of hair.

'Child of our time'

A gate ever so
conveniently
placed & a Zebra

waiting to be
ridden across
to the park . . .

where I sit
waiting for you
with the pigeons

while a lady with
several moth-eaten dogs
and a large number

of cardboard boxes
in a wheelchair,
waits perhaps for

the traffic to stop
roaring along
Piccadilly – your

blue sunblinds
look like eye
shadow round the

sad pupils they
contain, save the one
I was asked to leave

green in name and
troubled in colour
the park (or the Rivoli

bar) is full today of
sad nut cases and such
funny odd shaped trees

Camel

Erudite in surfaces, the obdurate
Stone, the too compliant sand, these he knows
Best, and spaces although inaccurate
With ifs and buts he comprehends, for those
Gifts is prized by those who know him best.

Our values differ with our deserts. We rail
As commoners this gothic thing in a
Bare compound, his tavern manners, the stale
Stews of his breath and keep veiled in purdah
Horizons that he never will outstare.

Sunset language and the celluloid ways
Of houri and Beau Geste, landscapes full of
Soul screen our long industrial days,
Those ex-rayed bones within the tinsel glove.
He knows oasis to be water hole.

No mirage fools his ancient alchemy,
That separates the stone from succulent.
Bored with the sophists of reality,
He wears the style of his environment,
We, the substance of our tattered overlord.

Poem for my father

Old fellow, old one,
    sing me a song out of the dark,
    a scullery one, and I'll beat time still
    on the tin bath.
    How clear you looked free of the work's dirt
    and gay with evening, your time for taking the air
    – you'd think breathing it was a work of art,
    my mother said.
    Sometimes before dressing, suds long at the elbow,
    you had me punch away at your bicep:
    always this strength; always the body,
    you tested everything on it,
    all life's fifty-year long shift:
    suddenly, you must lie down with its strange stillness.

Older, I thought all you left of yourself
    at home was a black ring round that bath,
    water down the drain,
    and me, cold leavings,
    to remind my mother bitterly of you.
    But do you remember sometimes on nights,
    out of the street's noise never got used to,
    you slept in my back-room, slipped carefully
    into the rumpled shape of warmth I left you there,
    each morning that ghostly crossing, you worn-out,
    me head-full of Donne, Shakespeare and Keats?
    – *Hyperion* to you was a beery windfall.
    Now I get you into bed and out of it,
    ashamed.
    My body was never my meal-ticket
    in the burrow of street and foundry under
    the rattling viaduct, the canal's dark bridges.
    Do you think if I could give you this strength
    I wouldn't?
    With finger-tip touch I steady your shoulders
    pretending you sit alone on the brand-new commode.

Old fellow, old one,
   sing me a song out of the dark,
   twenty years later,
   (must it be twenty years' late?)
   let the morning find
   that shared shape in the bed,
   – no more cold crossings for us –
   but the same flesh and warmth and need,
   a father, a son.

On buying London paving stones for the garden

I
Let us meet at the stones.
Along the hedge and under the big oak
the stones are stacked.

Their surfaces are rain-coloured,
with the colour of a light rain filtered
through twilights of lilac.

In the long-time London of their origin
they confirmed and threw back hard
hooves, wheels, footsteps

coming up staccato, retreating, a heel ground
on an endless wait. The lamplight
sank into them and was diffused.

Let us meet at the stones
arranged in their sloping library, tablets
of the once thunderous Law

which flows up in them now faintly and ebbs away –
or already laid out in preparation across the grass.
Islands should be joined,

there should be paths and the beginning
of processions.
When we look down upon them they deepen

like breathing skin.
They are discoloured with birdshit and hopscotch
and emblems like the trailing of blossoms.

When it rains they shine brown
like pebbles polished in pools.
Let us meet by the stones

and swear our tallest vows
and seal our promises
and lay fingers against the lipped earth

to set things in order,
slide covers on wells and allow the sleeping dead
to heave their laconic slabs.

Human beings need a plinth
of history from which
they can launch themselves

or a procession of paving stones
where they can walk about and stamp a little.

2
No need to sluice these stones
with a 'solution of cowdung in milk';
they read out their own stains
romantically from old silk
that is pigeon-coloured with years of rains
and footsteps and blind men's sticks.

Under the oak propped like tablets
or over the grass dropped like lids
they nevertheless have the private
look of an eye narrowed to shut
on what it sees, or a book
bound on the described deeds.

Yet only glance at their undersides
and you find all London's traffic has done
less harm to them than the dark fibres and clods
and chemicals rising under them;
they were fissured and scooped and gnawn
as they lay in their beds.

Now we set them one after another
with cement and sand till each fits
to a firmness. They smother
daisies and plantains down to the wild roots.
We walk ceremoniously and take the air
and hardly notice how heavy are the boots
on those doors of earth knocking to enter.

Angel

Beneath her bulk
The scales are swayed like God;
She dances on a pin
That bites an arc across both hope and pain.

For her, desire is only plus or minus.
At plus, she'll hide in corners
Gluttoning fudge in orgies of disgust
Till the hormonic balance of her cycle

Brings new resolve, drifts of ryvita crumbs,
Half-empty tins of grapefruit in the fridge.
The pendulum may swing towards size 12,
But her desire is based on self-deception.

She hides in fat as though it were a womb,
Suckles to quell a child's uneasy phantoms.
It is the fat that keeps her safe and pure
When pretty girls are summer on the streets

She dreams the lusting glances could be hers
For a few pounds dispersed. The stores plate-glass
Reflects her images. A regiment of women
Battle for consciousness;

But she will not force fate
By looking or by losing.
Too much to lose to see the truth
Too late.

Ask Hans

What do you remember?
                    I remember the copper dog
with saucer eyes galloping furiously at night
– a princess sat on its back – *& all because of one
stroke on a tinderbox!*

                    What else do you remember?
I remember the witch said to the soldier: 'Give
me the box *immediately!*' He drew his sharp sword,
struck off her head – I saw it roll on the road!

                    Anything else?
Yes. A prentice-boy ran past the prison – kicked
his clog at the window – brought the tinderbox
& received (I think) tuppence.

                    What did you see next?
I saw the King, Queen, Courtiers & some redcoated
buglers. The soldier (a rope round his neck) struck
One struck *Two* struck *Three* – & HUGE DOGS at once
(I positively saw them!) flung the Court in the air . . .

What next?!
                    I saw them sit 8 days at a feast.
They were happy as larks. I saw the princess
kissing & cuddling the soldier. I saw the huge
dogs glancing at the Courtiers & munching meat
& bones with glistening teeth . . .

                    (*I nearly said – but I won't! –*
'*What else did you see?*)
                    You're right about that!
There's no more to remember – unless I've missed
some of it somewhere. It's a very long time ago,
& who can tell?

                    Ask Hans!

Everything in the garden is lovely

Even the fat slug
That drags its belly nightly
Over dank paving
And into the heart of the lettuce
Is lovely.
And the seething myriads in the ant-hill
Are lovely.
The stealthy, disruptive mole,
The grubbing, wet-nosed hedgehog
Are lovely.
And the millipede,
The centipede,
The sexually reproductive woodlouse
Are lovely.
The dung fly and the dung beetle
Are doubly lovely.
The burying beetle, the emmet,
The devil's coach-horse, the dor
Are lovely.
Bean blight, leaf scab, club root,
Rose canker, cuckoo spit, wireworm
Cutworm, carrot fly, codlin,
Woolly aphis, apple weevil,
Leaf curl, algae,
Big bud, brown spot,
Rust, smut and mildew
Are all of them lovely.
And the flowers are lovely, too –
Nightshade, broomrape, henbane,
Love-lies bleeding and dead-men's fingers,
Viper's bugloss, red-hot poker,
Wormwood, woundwort, rue.
And the gardener himself is lovely –
With one eye on the stable clock
And the other on lovely nothing,
Flat on his back where he fell.
The lovely flies walk in his lovely mouth.
Everything in the garden is lovely.

The fly lot

The flies that crawled over his face
Variously
Were there
Part by accident and
Partly by design.
They were called green, red, blue, orange and black
Bottles;
Robber, dung, cleg;
Flat-footed, hump-backed, wolf.
Great glee had the gall midge thereon.
Danced merrily to the tune of no trumps the mosquito,
Anopheles or Culex.
Bombylius homed in astutely innocent,
so astutely as to be suspect.
Over the glazure of his eye skipped the winter-gnat.
Warmly down on his lips the hoverer,
Abdomen depressing, palpitating,
Alighted, pulsated.
And all over his wasted cheeks
In the channels and the tears
Swimming, crawling, burrowing, caressing,
Devouring – devotedly devouring,
Went all the rest, all you have ever heard of
And more –
Carrot, house, drain, horse, sheep-bot,
Ichneumon, currant, demoiselle, dragon,
Picture-winged travesties, the biters and borers,
Frits, fruit-flies, caddises, alders –
All the glittering militia out of the air
Paraded, manoevred on stubble and plain
Of forehead and jowl.
And look! They had won. See whom they
Had overthrown,
Small as they were but brilliant –
Brilliant every one in his own tiny manner.

Moles and men

Moles are creatures living under the ground.
Deep.
Dark.
Down under.
Men are creatures living on the ground.
In houses.
In huts.
Their homes.
Men earn their living from the ground.
Toil.
Tears,
Time spent.
But there are some men below the ground.
Deep.
Dark.
Down under.
Like moles they burrow their way along
The ground,
The soil,
The earth,
For anthracite, nutty-slack, coke and coal-black coal.
Toil,
Tears.
Time.
And sweat, spent in getting all this for a living.
Why?
Why?
Why?
For other people's comforts – we all need coal,
For warmth.
For heat.
For power.
But what of the men striving under the ground?
Deep.
Dark.
Down under.
Do we think of them when we burn our coal.

For warmth.
For heat.
For power?
Do we think of the danger one piece of coal brings to
Men.
Miners.
Most workers?
They earn their living and in return get
Disease.
Dilemma.
Death.
In earning their living they are living their death.
Deep.
Dark.
Down under.
Moles are the creatures that live under the ground.
Miners are the men that die there.

Pressing the shutter
(for Hart Crane)

Standing in the road
he saw the skyscrapers
of the 'Ariel', for New York from Liverpool
– so narrow she turned over once
    sailing into the wind
    skysails dipping into the Atlantic –
and somewhere he stepped off
the back of a boat
quietly into the Pacific

you can see him now
pacing the dock road
at home maybe
in an alien commercial backwater
where the 'Hector' and the 'Ulysses'
leaning against the quayside
empty washing-up water into the dock
– the only sound

in thin fine rain flecks the puddles
and grey clouds drifting
tangles through the masts of ships
the 'Kawa Maru' moves up river
to load grain
following the clouds
– that Sunday in the sixties –
past laid-up ferry boats
past me with a camera
    as the taut ropes take up the slack
    flake wind-driven drops of water
pressing the shutter
becoming a photograph

The Major: an epitaph

No I never knew him – at least until
he died. His books were up for sale
and sitting at his desk I knew him then.
French windows opening on a squared-off lawn,
brown as an Indian compound,
a flagstaff with the halyards hanging loose,
a hedge of pampas grass
bordering the green canal,
the stagnant evening sticky with thunder flies:

The neat deaf housekeeper brought sherry on a tray
"To help you sort things out:
the Major would have wished it.
Quiet but firm and always 'on parade'.
The flag was raised and lowered every day,
the Major set great store by that."
And had he lived here long? "Just since the war.
Not old, but maybe sixty-odd.
He never married and his friends were dead."

Predictable books: Ian Hay; *The Hill;*
Buchan; *Tell England;* Kipling; Forster;
old Army Lists; Teach Yourself this and that;
no secret sex, all clean and decent stuff.
Good with his hands, but nothing definite,
fixed up some tricky switches for the light,
built his own desk and graceless shelves of deal.
On the Parish Council, sidesman at the church . . .
He should have been all right.

I found the diaries then. Useful for scrap.
And flipped them through to see
what should be burned.
Blank after blank; but here and there a date –
a Service Dinner, Legion Poppy Day,
Conservative Rally, village fayre or fete –
dry scattered bones to chart the way across

deserts of non-involvement . . .
Why foolscap size? That seemed to make it worse.

Back a few years and catching at the eye
a longer entry, numbered: *Points in Common.*
Our faith in God. Devotion to the Queen.
War service overseas. Then, *Sentiment,*
L for each other, also A and T. And last
Dislike of 'scum' government.
I should have burned them first.
And faced with his
My own life – nothing special – suddenly blazed.

When did it all start going wrong? Why should I care?
What use was pity now? Or love?
The time for that had finished long before.
He never married and his friends had died.
Why after twenty years should I still care?
Not out of pity, now, nor out of love;
guilt is the motive power – and fear:
how loneliness comes sifting silting down
and men are buried in it still alive.

Mr Skillicorn dances

Mr Skillicorn dances,
Mr Skillicorn dances,
He does it very well.
All by himself –
and when he falls,
– So slow –
he floats to the boards
on a wave of applause.

Mr Skillicorn's
arse hits the floor,
'Give us some more!'
'Dance like before
you fell.'
    'Encore!'
(You can't deny he's falling well –
tonight. Yes, – this was worth waiting for.)

We laugh,
but it's not funny at all.
Not any more.

Every time he hits the stage
we all of us cackle like hell,
but it wasn't funny when
the fat comedian fell.

We laugh for him.
He falls for us.
He strips
our tears
of laughter.
We've been
falling for
years, and
– after –,
Here comes another time,

Taking its chance,
'Dance, you fat bastard,
Dance, dance, dance, dance –'

Where's the rapport
we had before?
Mr Skillicorn you're
no longer fun.
(Outside the trains have ceased to run.)
We're willing to go home
if only you'ld admit you're done.
You're old, but the moon outside is still young,
the night is still young.

Mr Skillicorn dances.

Words

Even at dawn you expect me
to fill these pages,
detailing dreams and loneliness
as though that provides a meaning,
a contact our separation denies.

Impatiently, I wait for birdsong,
and as the streets
grope towards morning,
blind with electric and leaves,
your wakefulness crosses the distance,

interrupting my half sleep.
Stumbling, I find the words:
and they are neither right nor wrong,
but signs, leaving the darkness,
like raindrops when the rain is over.

Journeys

Waking in my room
you talk of cafes in Jerusalem
where we have never travelled
and stars fail to shine.
The painting on my ceiling
is your photograph,
a naked, blackbird dawn,
the lake blue as your eyes.

At the border, the guards smile.
You are moving somewhere
between my dreams,
but I cannot remember the town,
the flat, brown country.
Your voice reminds,
your hands explore a still wood,
cool in the leafed green,

your silence
is of birds and woodlands.
Always, we talk of Jerusalem,
the figures by the lake,
the small boats tiding into rain.
Our hands at last are still,
and our voices enter contentment.
We are journeys deep inside my room.

On trying to breathe in Rome

Clochards on metro vents, meth-drinkers, dredging
Dustbins at the Savoy, the wreck, who sleeps
On sacks in Michelangelo's emphatic
City gate regret these old imperial
Capitals have such disappointing weather.

Rome's forum stank of wet wool togas, Moscow
A flyblown Tartar fief, and even Paris,
Bitch among cities, such a lovely bitch,
Is cruel to the penniless, who smell
The truffles cooking, inside, for the rich.

They move ahead to find a better site:
Tomorrow, an island on a useful river.
In other places, roses grow for ever.
Only great Alexander chose his city
Well, but the sacking Arabs moved to Cairo.

In those Hesperides, cits lie stupefied.
Siestas last all day, and women melt
To mounds of vanquished flesh; their men become
Vindictive and morose, as if they lost
Yesterday's wages, betting without pleasure.

Empire is solecism: tourists bake
On soporific beaches; only deadbeats
Batten, like soldiers, off a supine city.
Diplomats lose their way in architects' dreams:
Islamabad, Brasilia, Canberra.

A lovely bitch will show a greenhorn more
Than dancers in Tahiti: lack of breath
Outwits their sunburnt stupor. This encampment
Of thieves is our hereditary city,
Where terror may be disciplined by pity.

To Euros Bowen

Euros Bowen came to read
his poem.
We to listen and acclaim.

So first there were the speeches
from his hosts.
'Honoured, privileged and glad'
They boast.

Euros had an impish look,
Holding a copy of his printed
book.

Sometimes he would cup his ear,
As if beckoning come near.
But we sat, shuffling our
embarrassed breath.

And he continued,
Slightly deaf.

Two old ladies at a recital

Having once read that
'man does and woman is'
I do not remember it.
For these women are both old,
It being long ago that their
last loves were absolute.

Perhaps all manner of things
flow to them now from the keyboard,
For it is a man playing
Keeping our side of the bargain.

In a pause, I see one face.
It is creased by a life of
surprises.

I look down at my own hands.
What irony this music plays,
For lives of flesh intestate.

Father in the thirties

Where were you father in the
poetic thirties?
In the humped up days of Auden, Spender, Lewis,
Empson and MacNeice.
They were all safely back from Oxbridge
and down on the starting blocks.

And where were you father?

I know you had a little car
That's how you met mum, stopping on
the Eastern Avenue.

Whilst pens scratched for Spain and sanity
Your answer stood for itself.

You caught up with them at the edge
as a peace was lost.
(The predictions I concede are theirs)
But you, unmoved, buying petrol when told,
said 'who cares'.

Miss Charlotte

Miss Charlotte has taken her place
but not at table, where her older sisters sit
straight-backed and solemn, while Papa says grace.
Charlotte's in the parlour, a smile upon her face
and her hair not quite as Nana used to do it.

Her cheeks are too pink and perfect
like the bisque complexion of her favourite doll
whose soft and rigid body she protects
with one gloved hand. Anne and Jane come to pay respects;
they curtsy from table and tiptoe down the hall.

Her sisters' lips are pale and prim,
returning Charlotte's rosebud smile. The three girls stare
at each other, all so strangely dressed and slim
in newly tightened bodices. The crêpe on the brim
of Jane's hat comes loose in her fingers; Anne repairs

the hat and says they're worn no more
than once and then we have to give them all away
and isn't it a waste? But Jane is sure
she heard unfamiliar horses in the driveway
and saw two black dressed men go round to the back door.

The Comforter

This morning, admiring a newly opened rose,
his shadow crept over my shoulder
and the birds uttered warning cries.
A reminder that my country is far away
time to begin the journey home.
I have grown fond of this place
this enclosed garden
with overgrown roses and clustered wisteria,
my many loves,
but he has revealed himself in dreams
his embrace is comforting.

     He has followed me through the streets,
     sat near me in the train,
     behind me in my room.
     Always loving.
     Since my birth he has observed my growing,
     looked closely into my living.
     Always impartial.

The rowan berries shine in the setting sun
clouds are gathering across the fields
impressing me with urgency.
Days drop with the leaves
are trodden into the earth – vanish.
When I ask him: 'Now?'
he ruffles my hair with his long fingers.
He waits.
Time to start back, a long walk,
and much will have changed.

Hoofprints

The legend was always here,
at first invisible, poised above the hill,
stiller than any kestrel. Idle hands
carved hoofprints on a rock
by the hill path. The legend, venturing nearer,
breathed warm as blessing. At last
men recognised it. A magic horse
had leapt from hill to hill, they said,
the day the valley began. Could they not see
his prints, that had waited in the rock
till guided hands revealed them?
From the unseeable, legends leap.
In the rock of our days
is hidden the print of miracle.

Salvador Dali at the Hollywood Bowl

On the movie set intelligent tranquillized lions
purr like warm cameras. The swooning blonde,
sprayed a marigold bronze, sinks into her mould
of jungle mink. On a magnetized pillow
gold tresses arrange their rich molecules in waves:
the moist face of the director beams like a sunflower.

Padding home past the used rocket lots
where ancient nose-cones gleam a cold pewter,
the lions yawn gold-plated dentures.
Somewhere, a black bat, impaled on a radar reflector,
emits small bleeps on screens in concrete caves.

In the creative stillness of the director's palace
lions crunch the cold leaves of frozen sunflowers.

The beach at Trouville
(after Boudin)

For them,
it's a blue day
years before we took
blue sadly.

For so long,
the parasol has stood
open and,
in the blue day,
fading slowly.

Her blue dress
folds over the black rock:
her sister's
grows damp on the sand.

The men wear flat caps
and no-one appears to be smiling.

It's a blue day
years before
blue wept.

The odd man out
on the left of the group
looks away
and ahead
toward a pencilled, blue horizon.

Lost tongue

Penzance, they say, meaning
Holyhead, for this was
Celtic land.
　　They heard
bells calling to Mass
under the Atlantic –
lost land, lost tongue
last spoken by Dolly Pentreath
these two hundred years:
Durda dhawy, God grant
good day to you, and the reply
Durzona dhawy, God speed
to you.
　　Turn over the pages
of the old grammar: whole verbs
embalmed, their moving parts
perfectly still, nouns
packed tight as mackerel
that slithered in the net
of no dictionary, quick
speech of the Three Maries
at the tomb, the clifftop *plen
an gwary.*
　　Question the surface
of this land where only
place names are left: Marazion
because Thursday is market day
Carclaze of the bluegreen rock
Lanivet, Gwennap, Botallack –
fishing villages, tin
towns, so many broken
chimneys marking the deep
abandoned structures.
　　We have
gone on: but all has not been said
as witness overhead
the dumb and screaming gull.

The lecture tour

Determined to impress
I carry a brief case
It contains my toothbrush.
The notes for my speech are in my head
And I have a small head.
But if I put the notes in my brief case
And the toothbrush in my head
Who knows what will come out of my mouth.

Handy and uncuffed

Look at your hands, toolmaker's daughter,
Hold them up, arrest their skills;
Seldom muslined in milk now, yet
Draw them from dough, scrub off the earth,
Leave the seam to another spinster –
Or if no seven-morninged darling
Let keys be silent, files closed,
Pen capped, brushes rinsed out.

Stand them at ease then, and whether
Elegantly greased and varnished, or
Calloused and grimy in the cracks,
Ringed or beringed – interrogation
Reveals the world's peacemakers:
Home-making pro's of Vestal devotion
Who far outnumber the outdoor crowds
Of marching and demonstrating feet.

Why brood or rage for what you cannot?
However often mopping up blood
Spilt at entrances, half-times, exits,
They will never have to shed it.
These workers can't be told to strike
A hair on any head, and those who
Wash the floor and pick up the pieces
Earn the right to say 'Don't drop it'.

Contemplate the childhood of freedom.
Who uses spoon and scalpel, chooses
Rubber or kid, or lies lap-idling
As each dandled idea grows?
Why cuff them in a high-rise world
Behind knocked doors from nine to five?
(It was unusual for Mrs Fish
To speak severely to her daughter).

The Duke is dead

Today we buried the Duke in an indigo mood,
Surrounded by ten thousand tributaries
And Ella's voice. We who have heard the best –
Can hear it still, can marvel that the child
Of another century welded the worlds of jazz
From Cotton Club to Cathedral.
Old bloodhound, old gentleman, old sleepyhead,
We gave only your body to the dead.

Three positions

1   The chair position (for Keith Vaughan)

In the centre of this room
a chair
in the chair
a man
in the man
a certain position

a position inappropriate
to dancing or dying
but adequate.

White room, white
chair and a man
heavy with himself;

the sky there
almost at a point
where he does not
need the sky

as though God gave
a pattern and left
each one to make
reality.

Chair, room and man
hold each other
like an atom

in a question
of whether to
disturb the world
or masturbate.

2   The couch position (for Francis Bacon)

Red walls, red couch
and a raw figure
as though the flood
had just gone.

Looking in on edges
which cannot contain
where we flow
into red walls
red couch and meat.

Along the street
clean traffic goes
lights blink on
and a dog barks
for a lost note.

We cannot choose:

looking out we watch
others looking in,
like voyeurs
down the throat
of living.

3   The bird position (for Paul Klee)

I have said
I will make things
this way

I am not good
at this kind of
statement

am more likely
to eat paint
than paint precisely

would rather cry
at music
than describe it.

The craftsmanship
of God
is His mystery

saying this
I know
it is not enough

yet I say
I will make things
this way

as though God
on his eighth day
will make a reason.

November

Long summer loosens now
the speedboats and the girls depart
shaved stubble shows its skull
and the first mists start
a comfortable loneliness

Dead oaks align themselves
like markers on the marshes
and flat farms, and docile ducks
with winter coughs
sound storybook alarms

Wait. It will happen.
Watch the way the sky expands
not reaching out but running from
small hands freezing as
they squeeze prayer

Behind barns and breakwaters
some corner of the weather
slips to where
the North sea sways
weed and shingle

Offshore a seal pup barks
and beaches itself upon rough sand
his slashed belly baring
like a broken hand
this year's sacrifice.

Recollections from a death bed

Waiting circa 1949, in the little waiting-room
Beside the single track, with the small stove crackling,
Reposed on a bench, reassured by a verified connection,
The journey onwards going twenty miles
To a destination feeling remote (no seagulls
Floating in this far from the unreachable marshes)

He listens to the quiet and contemplates distance:
The long miles slowly to go in the two carriages,
Then the light in the wrinkled panes of the door,
And the known face opening and greeting.

Three hours before he had been: a philosopher,
Recounting in a lecture *things we can be certain exist,*
The other side of the moon, for example, which cannot be seen
But may reasonably be inferred. An hour and a quarter
To wait.
    A low fence exists, he sees it, on the far
Side of the track, and a dimmed field beyond, leaves lying
Dulled by the rain, circa 1949 and autumn.

The stove, for now, inextinguishably secure;
And hard corner-arms to repose on, in the straight seat
In the somewhere surely-coming small train;
Then all the villages ahead, reached singly,
The place with a market, the one with a harbour . . .
Trees brushing the windows, darkened grass along cuttings,
A known face of the moon veiled above the coppice.

And the little room was secure at the time,
And stayed so, carried in the mind when the station
Closed and the track was wrenched up, and the
Stove broken out of the wall.
Life, Elizabeth, he said, *is certain to get*
Imperceptibly faster and more brazen. And later, *You,*
Were always some distance to reach, but
Today, how everything feels too close, is much too seen.

We die, these days, of the obvious and the near.
We die of the marshes towed to the caravans in
Half-an-hour.
  He is dying today, in a twelfth floor room
With a high steel crane veering outside the window, higher.
But delay, blessed delay, yet. Thinking time. An hour
And a quarter to the end.
   Dear Elizabeth. Just to say
I shall come by train in the usual way.
I shall have to wait at Charnham for contemplation.
I ought to be with you by just after five o'clock.
Don't trouble to meet me, I have little to carry. And

It is a mere ten minutes' walk from the station.

In a long chain

I think my work is important, I am a link
In a long chain.
I had to have the training for it,
And I had to dirty my hands.
They ask my advice when they want to know
    what would be best.
I might move up even higher, in time.

One Sunday, I woke up shouting. She said,
What on earth's the matter, we're supposed to be
Going out to dinner later; or rather lunch.
I dressed, and played with Lynda, and
Felt a bit better.

I was called into the office from the shop
Floor. 'Mr Fletton, up from London, wants to see you.'
But I was hearing the mutter-mutter,
The kind-of giggling noises inside the machines

Through four thick concrete walls.
I could not read the words in front of my eyes.

I know, but for me, that none of the stuff would get
    carried
As far as the door of the shop, let alone
Get onto the containers and out to the port.

She said last Thursday, you haven't said a thing
The whole evening.
I said no, I've been watching.
. . . I couldn't name a thing I'd seen on the screen.

Today is vital, people are relying on me
To get ten thousand packages out on time.
I am part of a chain, a link, they ask my advice.
I open the front door. After the wind,
It's a lovely cool morning, and sun;
Very bright.
The keys of the Toledo are clenched wet
In my right hand. And I don't move.
I am standing shaking. I am standing, shaking.

Inventory of his briefcase

Bright green apples in a
Brown bag,
A small black and white
Italian electric lampswitch in a
Brown bag.

Brown zip fastener, trouser length, as yet
Entirely unattached, in a
Brown bag.

A scarf of scarlet wool,
A spotless handkerchief of Bowater paper,
A pencil of cedarwood.

Six sheets of jellygraphed fruitfulness from the
Tomato specialist who lives in Luton.

Blue spectacle case with lid and hinge and spring containing
Black spectacles, in reasonable safety and comfort.
A second spectacle case, but O, so different!
Having neither lid nor hinge nor spring, being
Differently constructed, and containing
Nothing.

Brown Scotch recording tape
Bearing melancholy Scottish ballads such as
The Unquiet Grave, Lord Randall and
The Demon Lover,
Who stamped his foot through the boat's bottom,
When both he and she went down.

Red plastic case containing foolscap
Property of the Crown (behold the insignia!), and
Covered with closely spaced
Blue lines or
Bars.

The 'Captive', Part 1, by
Marcel Proust (deceased),
Brown diary for last year, obsolete, naturally,
Brown diary for this year, partly unused.

Red tipped danger matches in a
Yellow box, on which is quite discernible
Though badly printed, a small
Red house or
Ark.

Trees

They were talking about trees in the office,
and I was sneaking a look at an anthology of poetry,
and I came across this poem in which someone asked
if the poet had written a tree poem. It was a good
question, and I thought about it myself. I'd written
a couple of poems which mentioned trees, and one
in which a lady lived in a tree, and there was another
poem which said that you can't talk to trees.
You can talk to people, or at least some of them,
but not to trees. I mean, who'd want to lie in bed
next to a tree and try to make conversation afterwards?
It's bad enough with certain women, but a tree!
And it would probably be Autumn and the bloody thing
would be shedding its leaves all over the sheets,
and that's even worse than a woman who sheds tears.
So, I thought, no, I hadn't ever written a proper tree
poem, and I was pretty sure I never would, then I
had another look at the poem in the anthology, and
I realised the poet wasn't writing about trees,
not really. When I listened in to the conversation
in the office, they weren't really talking about trees,
either, but outside the window the tall, slim trees
were gracefully swaying in the wind, and I started
watching them closely, and thinking that loving
a tree might not be too bad a thing, after all.
I wasn't really thinking about trees, of course.

A stone wounded
(*for Gully*)

A giant stone wounded
by the air that rides it
bucks up and down on the crest
of our gazes, up this hill
we scale, towards it.

You, light on my shoulders,
small hands on my ears
cupping me with sound waves:
'Daddy, this is a *mount*ing.'
Yes, Gully. A mountain.

And so it is, your first own
mounting, out of your
babbling times, shared below,
as high over gorse and heather,
speech is a second sharing.

There: the great boulder's slow
wasting of dust into time
as air rushes through time and
time rushes through air
moistens eyes now

that look in and through me
to my own gone childhood,
right in at that sea-deep
place you just came from, I had
forgotten was still there:

its gigantic stone body all
core, so radiant
through time it can only scatter
its dust on the quick invisible
air, unendingly

reckless, transparent And you
are the boulder, and I am
the mountain. This is the real
dispassion: every other wound
is darkness and death mounting.

Once, Gully, there shall be
no more hills or opaque
heartless stones eroding
or bobbing eyes like ours among
these presences, or echoes

of ghostly seas in our ears or
blabbing tongues in heather
like these, but only your
radiance of a stone wounded,
not by the surrounding air,

but the starry brightness its
own core discharges.
Come on, down we go. Pick
your mother some heather.
Yes, this is a mountain.

(1973, Snowdonia)

On the raft

I didn't know about her fear
but touched it,
pulling her on my lap
and having her slip off deftly,
quick as a fish.
Lying on the hearthrug's raft of solitude
she looked abandoned, but it was a safer thing
to float on, wafted by heat and dreams,
hair strewn on the thick river of sex,
raising her head slightly to sight her breasts
in a kind of wonder at their effrontery.
Her eyes rippling over them began to love them:
they weren't naked but they could have been,
baring themselves by an imperceptible swaying
of the boat. The faint stir of her thighs
drew me helpless to the deep water.

A tour of the medical school

As, intense monolith,
The stone will dispose a ground
Of silence, so these are concerned with
It in an airy room

Such a mouth, set upon
Such obtuse reverie,
Endures, I suppose, as long
As the air's oddness, its sweetness

And limp, like a fallen pear,
There, at the long extent,
Lies, amidst dry hairs,
Flat, man's empty purse

MacLeod's Maidens

'Yet the waves will not wash the feet
of MacLeod's Maidens for ever.'
Hugh MacDiarmid : Lament for the Great Music

1   Fledgling-gatherers
Mainlanders fleer. The eating
of guillemots is foul and foreign.
But there are no deer to gralloch
on St Kilda. The rock is sheer,
easier to climb barefoot.
Fulmars melt from the cliff face –
even a man of Lewis won't eat those.

2   The Lair of the Last Wolf
In the rank cave mouth, his sons
inside slaying the cubs, Polson
trammels the She-wolf, her tail
wound round his unsocketed arm.
'Father, what blocks the light?'
'If the tail breaks you will feel
its teeth.' His knife sinks upward.

3   Two Ruins
This day the Duke is evicting
the entire tenantry of Sutherland.
Not far from the Pictish Broch
a woman, more than a hundred
winters old, lies bed-ridden.
'She's lived too long, the old witch,'
said the bailiff. 'Fire the croft.'

4   The Colonel's Lady
'I do so love my little garden.
I've built it up from nothing.
The previous owner let it run wild.
"I loathe gardening," he said.
My dear, I couldn't have been

more shocked if he'd said
he was an atheist.'

5   The Duke's Museum
Stuffed with trophies ranging
from humming bird to elephant,
monuments to the taxidermist's
art and His Grace's eye.
In the shade of a capercailzie,
seven small brown birds labelled:
'Quail – once common, now rare.'

6   The Seventh Day After Culloden
Harry Rose, youngest foot soldier
in the Duke of Cumberland's army,
explodes his seed into a whore
and remembers Alba MacDonald.
Pus dribbles from the wounds
she ripped when he ploughed
her womb with his bayonet.

7   Rhôn Island
The night passed in a ruined croft,
backs frozen, huddled round embers.
The way back to the boat follows
a crumbling ledge – a stone falls
for three seconds. The dog cowers,
disbelieving, as Great Skuas attack.
On the beach we found a human foot.

Dozmary pool

A strained light as of steel:
   is it the sword's flight
   that colours all
this day, this moor, this utmost weather?
   Or the whiteness of an arm
   from the deep, the brandisher?
    The utterance of gulls'
blunt sight of earth and ocean
   is borne on the dulled iron
   wind swishing the lake
    against the sedges
savaged by the ruts of tractor tyres.

A bottomless mere, the cause
   thick grasping ooze
   and someone drowned,
the body never to be recovered:
   this then the cradle
of holy Arthur's passing?
    Rain spits
on the slant air across the tors,
   and the holiday traffic jollies
   past the Jamaica Inn
    where signs with care
direct one to Brown Willy and the Pool.

I stood on Brown Willy
   yesterday: territory
   only for the shaggy
cattle below me, but on the summit
   the mark of horses' hooves.
   One of Mordred's ministers?
    Or Merlin? Bors?
An over-obvious poetry, rather
   some jogging Jill or Jennifer.
   But comfortable afternoon
    smoothed all

doubts. And the stonechats sounded friendly.

    This morning's air
    prolongs the lack of mood;
       visitors arrive
in a Rover to view the haunted pool
    as I have come, as you,
    with an imposition of legends –
       the Sword, the Mere,
the Death of the Last King, the Wailing –
    conjuring an overworld
    of underworld remembering
       indigenous magic,
our native dialogue with space.

    On a far skyline, spectral,
    the clay cones of St Austell
       gatecrash the colloquy –
anachronistic witch-hills
    with the tantalisation of the abandoned
    shafts and engine houses,
       reliquary chasms
where we dropped a pebble bounding into quiet:
    bottomless indeed!
    No cob's creature
       stirred in the dark
at the summons of that idle sounding.

    And now the flat comfortable
    quilting of the pool's surface
       cries us quits,
gusts in the grass and the temperate contours
    of the mild moor in summer
    wrap up our unease.
       The valley slips
down to the sea and a midday meal;

next comes St Neots with the angels,
and the Devil's Cheeswring, then
   with luck
the Smuggler's Arms will deliver a cream tea.

Night call

Prised from sleep, I watch a disordered world
Collapse into patterns of dry meaning
On which I rub my tiredness. Two o'clock.
Five minutes since the telephone's rasp whirled
Into the crevices of sleep, cleaning
Out a dream's fading debris with the shock

Of consciousness. I drive the crumpled road
To town, the car's running incongruous
Through an empty land. Night bathes the aching
Temples of housing estates, cools the wood
Where a shrunk rife still trickles through porous
Scrap, old prams, cookers. The world remaking

Its battered heart. My lit destination,
The building marked POLICE, lies off the bend,
Its pulse the trust of honest men. I park,
Enter, announce myself to the station
Sergeant. He knows me. 'I'm sorry to send
For you. . .' His voice grinds on, without the spark

To fire interest. He knows these calls irk
And makes no pretence. A brief interview,
Arrangements quickly made and I clean up
Another job for the statistics. Work
Or habit, my actions bubble, then stew
Into a competence. Over a cup

Of dawn coffee, I scrawl out my report:
Runaway wife, an unchanged baby, myth
Of overblown detail. I shall require
More. Yet I know the case is of a sort
I'm bound to forget – this madonna with
A bruised face and her stinking messiah.

Elegy

My first funeral must have been the coldest
morning of the New Year, colder than
the death we came to celebrate.

The coffin at the altar lay like
the first primitive icon of a man,
hewn in despair from the heart of the living
tree where death flourishes as it will,
in a seasonal cycle unique to itself.

Out of the frigid stillness I heard
a phrase as pagan as viscera cut
for the gods: 'and bullocks at Thine altar'.

It was the very coldest day
and since there was a man
lying in my imagination in that wood,
it was not wholly human.

The wind was ice as
water down your naked back, the grave an oblong
mined from darkness, and its crumbling sides
edged round with raffia grass.

This green illusion
of summer lawns, and wreaths as colourful
as flowers, and the pristine plastic lines
of the lowered box deluded me:

I watched for the conjuror's hand that would come
out of the samite frozen air
and tap for the hiding assistant to rise,
houdini and lazarus.

There was no trick.
Frostbound flowers alone remain.

Tonight he's at rest, my memory
in the earth's immortal universe
where bulls adorned with garlands of fire
silently go their bloodred way
and at Thine altar give up life.

how mick jones of leeds united collected his 1972
cupwinners medal in considerable pain and showed
true grit and won a kiss from a girl with a fine sense
of occasion and a loving heart

down goes mick at the arsenal post
lays in sickening unfeigned pain
as the final whistle blows
his team–mates raise their joyful fists
but no salute from winner mick

and see the conquering hero comes
in weary climb to meet the queen
right arm with bandage to his side
strained mouth in wince and gasp

and see a girl lean out across the rail
to greet this manly man
gently take his blond head to her dark hair
in such a long long sighing kiss
of dreamy hollywood clinch
her perfume his cold sweat
drenched in sweet tenderness

and this is a moment to take to treasure
his pale face useless arm her loving heart
long after the graceless game
drab match of dour men
it is her kiss that burns

Sonnet at thirty-five

Though I eat less, my body's weight increases.
My teeth, for example, are baulked with lead
and the pressure on my liver never ceases
(how easily we trip before the dead!).
Pints subsume meals I miss or abrogate
and walks discharge my many spirits' due.
Where once I was early I'm now too late
to consider weights or balances of you.
And still it goes on: nails grow, hair lengthens
and overcoats put pounds on as we inflate.
If I say 'I'm here' I change the tense
and, changing, make new addition to my state.
What rattles in my head's less lead than age
or an excuse to measure words upon a page.

Proletarian poem

I am St Francis (Interim)
of Zandvoort on the sea;
a gang of Nordzee sparrows has
been hustling around me.

These birds brake bulbously before
they impudently land,
a clump of cheeping puffballs shuffling
just beyond my hand.

A smile at them; they squint at me
in cunning comprehension:
sceptical, without a doubt,
of my divine intention.

Five advocates flick missionary
portions from my plate;
our meeting is my festival;
my festival their fate.

Why don't they show humility
at my self-sacrifice:
poor sandwich sulking nakedly
without its upper slice?

I ought to take offence, I know,
at their ingratitude . . .
Are they not aware of the
morality of food?

They are but birds, of course – birds,
the idle darts of God,
spinning bewildered hieroglyphs
at the Old Man's nod.

As meaningless the bird's flight,
so meaningless the man
who flails against Omnipotence:
a failed Utopian.

To man so discontented
He will not grant His grace;
His eye is on the sparrow – if
the sparrow knows its place.

FOR THEM

Righteousness is picked to the bone.

NO WAY. NO ENTRY. NO THROUGH ROAD.
NO ADMITTANCE EXCEPT ON BUSINESS.
NO HAWKERS. NO CIRCULARS. BEWARE
   THE DOG.

PASSENGERS ARE NOT ALLOWED TO RIDE
   ON THE PLATFORM.
Prickles about the bell push at the back:
PASSENGERS ARE NOT ALLOWED TO GIVE
   THE STARTING SIGNAL.
Halfway down the lower deck
A light on either side that cocks a snook
In the safety of thick glass blisters.
SMOKING PROHIBITED. SPITTING
   PROHIBITED.

NO CASUAL CUSTOMERS. NO COACHES
   SERVED.
CLOSED EVEN FOR THE SALE OF
   WOODBINES.
DO NOT ASK FOR CREDIT: A REFUSAL
   OFTEN OFFENDS.
NO SMOKING. NO DOGS. NO PRAMS.

NO COLLECTION ON CHRISTMAS DAY AND
   BOXING DAY.
EMPTY. POSITION CLOSED. RETURNED TO
   SENDER.

NO CHILDREN. NO COLOUREDS OR
   CHILDREN.
NO CHILDREN, SORRY. BUSINESS LADY
   PREFERRED.
NO MID-DAY MEAL. NO VACANCIES.

PRIVATE. KEEP OUT.
THE PUBLIC ARE NOT ALLOWED TO CROSS
   THE LINE AT THIS POINT.
TRESPASSERS WILL BE PROSECUTED. BY
   ORDER.

NO UNAUTHORISED PERSON MAY OPERATE
   THIS HOIST.
PENALTY FOR IMPROPER USE £5.
NO SMOKING.

NO PARKING. PRIVATE PARKING. NO
   PARKING PLEASE.
CUSTOMERS' PARKING. NO PARKING
   EXCEPT FOR CORPORATION EMPLOYEES.
NO PARKING ON THESE GRASS VERGES.
NO WAITING THIS SIDE ON EVEN DATES.
DO NOT OBSTRUCT THE GARAGE ENTRY
   OPPOSITE.
IT IS DANGEROUS TO PARK ON THIS
   GANTRY.
NO LEFT TURN. ROAD CLOSED.

Cherub-shaped illuminations
Set a good example
By gazing at some prohibitions:
During the hours of darkness the iron rods
Supporting them remain invisible.

Stop picking at me.

Last invigilation
(for June Kelty)

Jittery, waiting with your dog,
you recognise my step. Emma welcomes me,
placid as an aunt, then curls up in a corner.
I switch on the light you do not need.

Training your fingers on the hieroglyphic script,
you trace the words I read. The raised cells
release their laggard meaning to your touch.
Sometimes you pause, check, then renew.

I note the time, start the exam proper,
and try to concentrate elsewhere.
For two years we have crossed roads together –
now I must leave you, kerbside, on your own.

On the table squats your tiny doll (for luck);
talc for your fingers; a steel clock primed;
and that primitive typewriter with six big keys
at which, straightbacked, you clatter, miles away.

Outside green is god. What is green to you?
'Grass is green,' you'd say. 'It doesn't go with red.'
Mechanical associations, skin-deep, vague:
For you the summer sun is grey.

Restless, Emma scratches, lousy with boredom.
Her bell jerks as she paws an ear. Her eyes,
mournfully intelligent, watch me as yours do never,
you of the doll's eyes, fixed to an empty stare.

The alarm shrills time. Your fingers throb.
The room is filled with an absence of noise.
Our two years together are suddenly past.
I am left trying to say goodbye.

Fragments
This is the use of memory:
For liberation
T. S. Eliot: Little Gidding

1
As the plane rises, we watch the island
receding from us until we can hold it
complete in the eye; framed by water, its farms,
bays, hamlets and promontories scaled down
to a comprehensible map below us.
So in the cutting room of the mind
we work to distance experience
to meaningful proportions, to link
those fragments of memory that make us.

2
Sundays are quiet. Across the railway
the row of terraced houses and the shop
on the corner, its air spiced by bread
and cough cure, a tin sign advertising
a tobacco not made for a generation.
The sharp click of heels on worn flags signals
a firmness of calf and thigh under bronzed nylon,
her morning errand bringing humanity.
to brick and stone due for demolition.

3
Some windows already boarded, as if
against a plague that will take all with it.
Even Provident Place is on the schedule.
One winter the canal froze and we walked it,
between locks, to the sound of church bells,
rejoicing in the temporary foot-way
and the luxury of gloves, until
called home by the smell of roast sweet on keen air.
Age is where places have immediate history:

4
The canal; a pub recalling conversation
that proved a turning point; a bend in the lane

a poem that might have been written;
or a bus shelter flesh
warm under a fair-isle jersey, her breasts
like plump birds in the nest of her brassiere.
Deep in us all the child whose habits
have survived fidelity and superstition,
and associations that will end with us.

5
A day's drive across the Massif Central,
that evening we dine in warm southern air,
the lights of the small town sufficient
on the verandah. Time drifts with the music
from a radio across the way
where a girl waters a roof garden above
a shop. Time for reconciliation
while tired minds eased by good wine find order
as observers of a place not our own.

6
From London fires spread a premature dawn
for suburbs where a thin rain of shrapnel
removes roof-tiles. For the young the advantage
of deserted streets and the blitz's black-out
to test the pulses of love. Recklessness or
a fine sense of values? As single-minded
the blood races towards the same warmth
to find a later reassurance
in the bonus of a winter's sunshine.

7
Besieged by snow the house stands sentinel
against the night, the young child's breathing
a tenuous hold on life. Experience
began with the first open blouse: the fruit
that expelled from Eden? Redemption
long bought in domestic fires, the spread of flesh

that estuary towards which all runs
to be lost in the ultimate ocean.
The tide stirs with the child in the cot.

8
In the bay ships nudge their way to harbour
the toll of bell-buoys a doubtful guide
in fog's peculiar claustrophobia
that gives even sound a new dimension,
and value to moments of clarity.
Then a face remembered. Though long past
and not known in any real sense of the word
the impression is there and its haunting tugs us,
We dare not look at our real wounds.

9
The end of a holiday seals off
another year. Younger, we hesitated
over decisions that closed doors. Now doors
slam behind us of their own accord.
Driving home at night we see on the outskirts
the darkness lit by fires where the town's waste is burnt.
We drive on to the security of street lights,
a familiar haven that has come
to take on significance.

The waiting

You want the wild yellow dog
to sniff the wide air
and wait

Here willows too must wait – the hanging tear-shaped
leaves of gumtrees
linger at a cliff's edge

Close-by the rocks are resting / red / gunmetal-grey
The purple hills watch patiently
the lower slope and olive-coloured leafage
rust-dappled in descending dots
A seagreen swell
is billowing at each one's base

Quietly in matted brush
small questing mammals hide and move
pausing perceive
the railway-line still waiting
under the firm green runners – each raised shoot
grown into a forest of sharp thin spears

Jointed and sheathing leaves
join with the bracteoles'
bright-blue and -red and mauve
wildflowers
with the interwoven bushes to make a thatch
high over oxidizing metal and half-buried sleepers

One way down

The scree empties down the mountain,
The stone under me constantly changes,
A stance of a sort, making it possible
Neither to stop nor fall headlong.
Amongst the glacial rubbish I can reach out,
Pick myself a piece, and make something of it –
A face of grey crystals, a good stone to hold,
An egg-shaped bird-body, the likeness of a skull.
It is hard to keep even the best ones
Or hand them over to secure bystanders
Watching from the edge of this paralysed torrent.
At a steep place I turn a somersault,
Land with a crunch, resume the long crumbling.
The floor of the corrie turns from a map
To a pelt of deer's-hair sedge and blaeberry
And stunted rowans rooting into the peat.
Now the rock-face rises to the full,
Rears over with an evening darkness.
The pools lie flat and shallow and black
As death, the ultimate absence of qualities.

Swifts

The swifts are back,
their flight on a knife-edge.
In the dusk we watch them
and feel at peace.
Their grace we take
as confirmation.

Our swifts are back,
we say, and touch now.
But their grace survives them,
whichever were ours.
And it hurts to touch you,
that wing of hair.

Whose love, my love,
in my hands tonight?
Whose spring again
in the bounce of your hair?
Our love is ghosted;
our swifts return.

Bachelor girl

The schoolgirls no longer schoolgirls responding secretly
To the warm, vibrating bench on the morning train,
And the new wives moaning at the pink plastic
Detergent bottles in the song-drenched supermarket,
And the young nun swaying slightly to the piercing bells,
And the bored typist fondling the marginal release key,
And the lesbian journalist on the *Christian Observer*
Writing shorthand love-letters to the severe headmistress
Of the high-class secretarial college,
And the acrid perfume of desperate souls
Prowling around my neat apartment, staining
The chastity of my hand-laundered sheets.
Under the hot sunlight in the sidewalk cafés
The sophisticated daughters of bankers and bishops
Accept the expensively-educated lust of air-pilots,
Stockbrokers, officers, and television executives,
With giggles smothered in Parisian cosmetics.
In the dispensary the chemist's assistant
Opens her white, hygienic uniform to cool
Her naked, moist thighs, and dreams of the cinema
Which will caress her trembling legs
With a Biblical Epic and an oversexed theology student.
O lunch-hours when shopgirls and secretaries
Explode into the streets to seek cut-price stockings and
    boyfriends;
O drowsy afternoons in the democratic parks
When the sailor on leave, or the insurance agent,
Kisses the part-time librarian, and they cling like
Beautiful animals on the bruised grass,
Watched by the sociological eyes of a small boy;
O evenings of yearning and stimulation
In the patient, parked cars near the churchyard,
Or behind the closed curtains of the motel bedroom,
Where I am seduced joyfully and frenziedly and endlessly
To the music of the sighs of all the women in the world.

John Clare, dismissed

A moon is at the edge
of cloud, a night storm gathering
when we have finished
our day's work. They let me have the wain

until I leave it empty
in the field where I lie down.
One end makes bars
across the heavy reddened face.

They say they will not have me
working here again. 'Moon-calf!'
one roared and flung away
my fork. Which keeps on touching

far away, small prongs without
a distant grumbling, the hurt
the darkness will sustain
upon its rim. Beggars bowls I can act out

with hands, but fens are endless.
It was because I could not trim
the load which fell. Imagining
is all my fault. I felt the wheat

should not ride true, the balance be
in emptiness. 'Let the sun
glare through!': as they all cursed.
There was a child who stared at me.

The route

As always I leave directions to you.
Above the driver's frown you hover,
gesture with your head then point.
A pale hand with a paler mark.

His destination one we might have reached
but myriads of small problems checked.
He'll soon reach gentle hills, and old dry-walling,
places where a few bleached stones outcrop.

Visible a moment
when you rest your hand upon the car,
a thin white line: half inch curve
where the whiplash caught you as a child.

A stranger going home and smiles all round.

About knitting

The spring wind clacks the hemlock needles
the sun blocks my shadow on the wall
while I sit, knitting.

You taught me to knit.
You would knit the whole winter through
binding off life-piles of squirrel-patterned mittens
for children to grow out of, style to outmode.

You have stopped knitting.
The sun and wind caught you
surprised on the half-finished sleeve.
A sudden sultry spring making you
drop stitches: wool's too warm,
the garment's ruined.
Bones knit, wounds can be stitched up neatly.
How can I unravel the mistake you let slip,
arrange the colours in their proper order,
put the recalcitrant yarns in their pattern again?

You will not let me.
You only let me
dance in your patterns, dangle from dream-bobbins
        All of us
in your life cannot rip you out of our crafting.
        We are picked up,
purled, slipped, passed over the knit-stitch,
at your will, you dead.

The spring wind clacks the needles together
against my will.
You have stopped knitting.
I knit for you.

The poor

The poor are still standing in the snow
Announcing their silence with cracked lips.
They do not move or go away
And wind unravels their gloves.

When the snow ceases to flurry,
Winter Palaces sweeten the distance
Reflecting the sun with a million windows.
But the decorated doors remain closed.

No one comes in wide sleeves
Carrying hot wine in a jade cup.
No one comes in thick uniform
Bearing rough blankets.

Canto fifty three

Naterk is my Mother
My Mother is old, failing.
The blind dog knows she's failing.
At night, too tired to eat.
I crack bones put slithers of marrow on her lips.
She swallows little. My son picks up the rest.

This morning, she refuses to ride on the sledge.
'I'm not dead yet' she says. And starts off,
To walk ahead of the team, already panting
like a walrus surfacing, her face red with strain
Before the days begun. And we with a long run ahead of us
Right down to the coast. She, facing a longer journey,
To that sea which has no shore.

No use telling her to ride again. Nothing more obstinate
    than a woman
Who knows she is dying.
For long I have thoughts of this day coming.
Now it is here, I'm helpless:
A boy again. Naterk is my Mother.

I hold the dogs back. Slow go, slow as I can.
Her feet are leaving no footsteps,
Just a shuffled trail where she drags along.
Now she is down on her knees again. I stop.
Tell her to ride. Pretends not to hear. Nothing as obstinate
    as a Mother.
Knowing she is dying.

I go pick her up. She makes me put her down.
'This is where I stay' she says.
'Now build Naterk a snow house.
She has to start that journey we all go on alone.
Build it here.' I shake my head. Naterk is my Mother.
Nothing as obstinate as a son
Who sees his Mother's dying.

I tell her with three days run
We reach the coast,
Where the white men come in black ships
give tea, tobacco and medicine, to make her well again.
And all that for the bear skin on which she is sitting.

She smiles. Says nothing, staring to mountains on the horizon
Where He dwells; He, the Father of all the Spirits;
He who breathes in reindeer through his nostrils
breathes out forests, waterfalls and stars.
I see she is frightened. She only smiles.
I turn away. Use the back of my hand.

Night: sweat runs down wrinkles in bark of her face
Her groans wake my daughter lying beside her.
Gets up and pulls five hairs from grandmother's head.
Puts them onto glowing ashes.
The smell of burning hair chases off evil spirits,
When the root of the hair's destroyed
The root of disease is, so we say, we say. . . .

Morning: she seems better. Eats, or pretends to.
Then sets off with her stick before I harness the dogs.
I do this slowly, give her time to get out of sight.
Then repack sledge to give more time
To claw her way up the hill.
Then slowly. The children ask: why so slowly.

When we catch up with her, she is sitting.
Her stick not in her hand: her hood up.
'You got a long way' I say 'We thought we'd never catch you.'
she turns on me. Her voice scolding.
'My son' she says 'Yesterday I told you my legs are too tired
    for this journey
I asked you to build me a snow house. You did nothing.
Do you want your children to see what you fear to see yourself?
Then build me my house.'

Then she gets up and brushes snow off my son's forehead
Who'd fallen, playing.
I take my spade from back of sledge and walk off.
'Why are we stopping here?' My daughter asking.
'Don' lets rest here. Why here?' My son shouting.

I build the house with blocks of snow
Pouring water over the cracks. When I finish it,
Begin another. This one smaller.
'Why are you building two igloos?' my son keeps asking.

It is dark again. My Mother goes to the sledge
Scrabbling through the skins. She chooses one, almost hairless,
Valueless, no white man wants. This she tucks under her arm.
All go into the first house. Eat. Children lie down. Sleep.
My wife sewing. My Mother stares into the fire. I poke it.
We don't speak. We don't speak of it.

Suddenly my Mother gets up. She tucks bare skin under her arm,
Goes to her place, takes a new pair of pants, new pair of mittens
From her sack. We pretend not to notice. She looks round the
    house.
She is looking with slow eyes at me. Then she goes over to
    the sleeping children,
Kneels and roughly pulls back hoods to their bare shoulder.
She bites them there. They wake crying
It is lucky to be bitten by an old woman. Anybody knows that.
'I am going now.' My Mother says. She goes out.
My wife sewing.

I wait to give time to lay her old skin on the floor
Of her little house, to put her new pants on, new mittens on
Then lie down ready dressed to go her new journey.
I, too, go out picking up a big knife as I leave.
With this I cut a block of snow to fit the hole she crawled through.

I see she's inside, now lying on the old skin, her old pants,
Old mittens folded neatly beside her.
Then I seal up the hole. Go back. Lie down.
My wife speaks to me with her hand.

Light at last. I have not slept, lying here
Thinking of her lying there,
Waiting for that which with all the time in the world,
Comes slowly.
Life is tiring. Death is restless. But it's the time in between
which is worst burden of all.

I am thinking of her now; listening to children playing,
the dogs barking. I harness the sledge.
She will know which strap I'm buckling now.
Now she will know which dog it is tangles his traces.
Now she will be crying. We're all children
When we lie there alone dying.
She hears us move off. Sits up. Calls out.
Cannot believe she is old, she is left.
Now cannot believe it is she who is dying.
Exhausted she lies down to sleep.
Sleep, deaths only mercy. Sleep the way
Death teaches us to die.

I drive dogs hard. Noon, stop to build igloo for family.
Leave them in it. Then hurry back alone to my Mother's house,
To do what has to be done. Drive the dogs harder.
Drifting snow already covers. Climb onto roof.
Take knife to cut small hole in centre so her soul
Can climb out, be free.

There she lies; knees up to her chin, a bundle of rigid rags
With new mittens on clenched fists.
I remember her as a young woman. . . .

It's a cruel thing to do
To bury your Mother alive. But what else can a son do
No way of keeping death from her?

I climb down drive dogs hard again, stopping here and there
to slur sledge track with my boots.
Let death stay with her now, not be able to follow us.
With her in his arms, he should be
briefly satisfied.

The animal-lover

Good dog, Argos,
bedded in the shit,
good dog, easy:
can you hear him yet?

Up the beach he crunches,
relishing each stone;
seaworn nostrils pinching
the special salt of home.

Lie quiet, Argos –
running sores and fleas –
dying to infect him,
hatefully diseased.

He wants no commotion:
he's had enough of fighting.
His wife's as chaste as ever:
he might just invite them

to stay a little longer
till they've heard all his tales.
Really, all he wants to do is
flop down like a sail.

Good dog, Argos,
rag and bone and mud.
Good dog, greet him,
change his mind to blood.

When you growled to see them
make themselves at home,
did they try to win you
over with fat bones,

until they came to call you
damned thankless sneaking cur?

Did you choose neglect,
eking out the years

until the moment – now –
when he passes by?
Lay back your ears,
judder your rump: his eye

flickers – my dog! Argos ! –
jerk your rusty tail,
let your last gasp trigger
his colossal kill.

Lie quiet, Argos:
although, at his side,
you may jog no longer
he will stand supplied

with your old companions:
the bow, the bristling sheaf
of arrows, like a mouthful
of unfailing teeth.

He will draw the bowstring
taut, and deftly –
good dog, Argos –
unleash it, swiftly.

Sardinia

Peninsula where no-one went;
In its garrigue we hid our tent.

In some more yards the waves would leach
An island, sieving the isthmus beach

To where we float. The water slips
Cooler fingers round our naked hips

As we swim down. Suddenly we see
A vast wall move from the verdigris,

Cutting us off, glinting like distant spears
Smacking perception with unknown fears

And now, a silver curtain weaves
Through the sunpleats of the sea, and leaves

Of ten thousand passages no tracks.
Before the shore, the sun has dried our backs

To salt as dry and white as bone
To salt as dry and white as bone.

On running into old friends in somebody's novel
(viz., Richard G. Stern's *Europe, or, Up and down with Baggish and Schreiber*, published New York, 1961)

Inside the margins of a book
through the screen doors of ink
you find yourself among explained people,
when you imagine from one clue, or two,
people you cannot bore or smell,
who will not love you or seduce your friend.
They have names out of telephone books –
Baggish and Schreiber –
but of course they are not real.

How strange then
on a train in there
to meet someone you know:
one who remembers moonlight on our faces –
enough to read you by
if I could read –
our hesitation near the shadow;
and that one's voice; that dog, that awful dog;
and him, the man without a neck,
whose grandfather invented
telephone insulators.
There they all are, characters, helpless now,
but looking round at the compartment door
when Baggish enters,
as if they could sense me,
invisible but behind his back,
a recognisable reader.

And then, how strange for them, now –
but maybe they're all dead –
to read these lines, to feel those days again:
Jocrisse, the burnt mountains,
the mysterious German gardener,
Caval-en-l'air, the dead snake in my bed,
the weeks of cherry-blossom-exclamation!

So afterwards, on your way to Austria,
for the cheap shoes,
you must have met this novelist on your train,
while I met Giuliana and the Sheriff.

Perhaps if you read this you'll write me
offering as you did before, a job –
teaching (a great-great-grandson, this time)
Latin and algebra.

Thank God I'm real only –
at least I can ignore a letter,
put a frame round it, hang it up
without answering: but you,
whenever I feel like looking,
remain there in that book,
rocking along in the train for me to stare at;
outside, the mountains of 1951.

The last journey

Old family cars have a certain appeal.
Families get fond of them. Cartoonists
love to draw them with big round eyes.
Also, of course, in a way they are monsters –
like other poets, dogs in particular, they are polluters,
fuming up the high streets. They kill people.

All cars, too, are rooms on wheels; and have witnessed
acts of love, arguments, affectionate banter,
the behaviour of children. Like animals, like us,
they deteriorate with time. The earth renews
but they do not renew. A licence in April
brings no bright resurgence of power and beauty.

If you've been fond of one, it's hard to think of it
chained with battered others on the big transporter,
cracked windows, dented like a toy
by a termagent two-year-old; the words Old Faithful
come to mind to remind us of the so many journeys.
Turner felt the same about the Fighting Téméraire.

Home truths

What the censorious wives,
the ones who throw words like knives,
have never understood
is how it's the hen that pecks –
not the hope of better sex –
makes men leave home for good.

By ravenous sirens misled
into an alien bed?
Not so. The better lay
might be in domestic sheets
and it's not for erotic treats

husbands go on their way.

A truly nasty remark
in the conjugal dark
can act as a potent spur –
he only wants to escape,
in any form or shape,
the flying of the fur.

He longs for a different diet –
a little peace and quiet;
and to be always told
how he's an also-ran
and really hardly a man
makes him feel very old.

The Other Woman waits,
and she's not hurling plates
or thinking him inept
or running a permanent quiz;
it's him, just as he is,
she will accept.

The stir of a woman's tongue
has got some good men hung
in more vindictive days.
Trouble is what it stirs –
not his alone, but hers –
there's death in a phrase.

Last movements

In Old Master music in sonata form,
by Mozart, by Schubert, you always find,
after the sadness and the emotional storm
that moves or maddens the listening mind,
strumming the nerves like the strings they play,
that four, five or six will make the mood gay.

This is a convention, we know, of course,
and a wistfulness in the rumti-ti-tum
might be detected; the sorrow's force
gives way to the logical musical sum,
as vigorously, brightly, the players bend
to a dance where unhappiness comes to an end.

But perhaps there's thanksgiving concealed there too
for a life that also contained some joy,
a kind of reminder for me and you
that nothing's pure, and without alloy
nothing. The dark swallows up despair
as well as hope – says that rustic air.

Victory on Ship Street

A bomb-blasted pub!
Another blow
      struck
for our very own corner
on Devils' Island!

Stabbed a thousand
times by flying glass
two wee girls
in Halloween dress
      burnt
to death as witches!

Enemy encounter

Dumping (left over from the autumn)
dead leaves, near a culvert
I come on
      a British Army Soldier
with a rifle and a radio
perched, hiding. He has red hair.

He is young enough to be my weenie
-bopper daughter's boy-friend.
He is like a lonely little winter robin.

We are that close to each other, I
can nearly hear his heart beating.

I say something bland to make him grin
but his glass eyes look past my side
-whiskers down
      to the Shore Road street:
I am an Irish man
      and he is afraid
that I have come to kill him.

Someone you know on the beach

Perhaps I am this fellow, with his feet up resting
By the sea,
With his feet up, flicking now and then
The sand-flies or the sand,
But usually
Still, and the legs too, stretched stiff,
Composed as if in relaxation,
Tanned, hairless
Under the many-coloured shorts,
That would like to be Tahitian or Hawaiian,
Or some jazzy place where the fun is,
And the bare torso, curved as if
In relaxation
On the snazzy-coloured beach-chair
(Called 'holiday' in the ads, but not there
Shown alone there, not on a brown beach,
Alone with the kelp quietly resting as it does
Half-asleep always asleep in the waves),
And the face, twisted a little on one side,
As if in relaxation,
Looks, yes looks frowning, if it is not the sun,
Or squinting,
Trying perhaps to make out a meaning
Somehow in that image in front of him,
Sun, sand, brown kelp, and his feet up
By the sea,
The ever-hurrying sea, the restless, the alien one.

Night-music

1
I listen to music I haven't heard for fifteen years
and remember every note. As if a conversation
paused for a moment and the moment became a lifetime
and no-one noticed. In such familiarity
across years which of us two is stranger?
My 1959? My 1974?
I can't tell who asks, who refuses to reply.

2
I wear head-phones. In the black window I see
a man wearing equipment for a brain operation.
It seems to work. Each half of my head slowly
rediscovers the lost art of independence.
And other losses too, when I take them off:
silence to the right, silence to the left, and I hear both
knowing how there is no way of turning my back.

3
Morning. First snow. Silence from the fields and woods.
I feel warm in it, though the music is coiled
away in silence, though each word said is muffled
by the soft ghost of silence clinging to it. The winter
sun is late yet the room is full of a pale light
as if news had just come of someone's death
and no-one has begun asking questions, and no-one answers.

Runmarö

An ice-age boulder, gross
solitary of the forest.
A boat in the grass, roped
in black plastic, for committal.
A collapsed smithy, the bellows
the hard-worked lung.

These survive while the forest
quietly absorbs its own,
generations of mushrooms
and 'Swedish soldier' flowers,
houses awash to the eaves
and Baltic family histories.

A photo: we're green and brown
in a brown and green world.
We're speechless, half open
mouthed, for air. A radio
sits on a bright table,
an ice-age marvel on display.

Equinox

Heads down now the hard weather's come, the kids
snap out of school. At four the greengrocer
stacks his pavement spread, trolleys it inside.

No sunset. The sky at chromatic north.
No cloud, only this north wind of colour,
the sun's recessional, the equinox,
when fire and brimstone behave like angels.

Low, impermanent as a shanty-town
lie the bare precincts, the dormitory streets
to these trebles of gold, this green alto.

Over the playing fields, at the street's end,
the cold declensions of October light.

The Tyger

Tyger Tyger
I remember you prowling
across the dining room table
you snarling, it curling its clawed feet

your stained walnut teeth
like a chain smokers
frightened me, the child

watching your dark snarls
and polished tail waving in anger
I hid in the corner of the room

Now I think of you being lovingly carved
all those years ago in a garden in Italy
your bad temper slowly emerging from the naked wood.

Lancia with electric windows

In 1932 you – spectre of the Fitzgerald Age –
crossed the Alps in panting Lancia
electric windows wide open
garrulous Italian chauffeur addressing mountain flowers

Uncle David's enormous ears sweating
under straw hats laughter
and the jolting of full stomachs

'Our happiest days', she said
speaking languages, visits to cathedral vaults
with potential giggolos and tea with the countess
white gloves on a silver tray, endless meals in Budapest

Ah, the closed restaurants of Europe,
the gastronomic itineraries of memory

And now I come to peer through the windows
of dead day trips to lake Lugano.

The Egyptian Room,
Metropolitan Museum of Art

1
A falcon hovers,
settles. Is petrified.

2
Behind perspex
a stone falcon
stares ahead.

Is crowned;
is a god.
Between his claws
a man. Petrified.

3
From without perspex
a Negro custodian
observes falcon and man.

Poet in winter

Outside the house the pools are crazed with ice
That little boys in wellies like to smash
With early sex destructiveness that will turn to nice
Little girls, the virgin outraged and the pash
Of self destruction combined with the lash
Of recrimination when tears are shed,
Leading finally to becoming wed.

As I was saying before all that stuff
That Freud put in our heads, its fucking
Cold outside. The birds can't get enough
To eat, they live off the wind looking
For all the world like scattered bits of rag fighting
Each other for the slightest crumb.
The fox upon the hill is dumb

With the pain of nights that kill
And leave the morning white and sharp as glass.
I of course can eat my fill
Of murdered beasts, stuffing myself to pass
The time while waiting for the crass
Stupidity of love to come to light.
Craftily setting snares for young Miss Right

Who almost always turns out older and sadder
Than my imagination could conceive,
And leaves me in the end great deal madder
Than before. But I've a lonely ice breaker up me sleeve
And out there on thin ice I can achieve
A smashing time that puts me with the greats,
Even if they do say, he masturbates.

Stringing words together in the cold like Eskimos
With bears teeth to brighten a dull life
Is only therapeutic I suppose
Keeping me off the streets and out of strife,
Affording me a little comfort on the knife

Edge of a world thats nothing if not funkey,
And cold enough to neuter a brass monkey.

But string I must with patience and with guile
Hoping no one will catch me at my one deceit,
Fiddling away here alone while
The real world falls down around my feet
And better ones than I are forced to keep
Appointments that they'd rather not,
As always, Komm Heiliger Geist, Herre Gott.

So with the New Year here and resolution made,
Despite the cold, despite the lack of cash,
For ever and ever to avoid the grave,
Amen to this and amen to the crash
Of western european civilization. Don't stash
Your living underneath the bed
You cannot take it with you when you're dead.

The death of Mussolini

They were not far from the frontier.
Although April was warm to the touch
His heart was colder than a villa
Shuttered against looting, and rags
Of glory exposed his naked terror.
Hadn't he told Clara he would rather
Put his fortunes into cold storage
Than bury himself, like the Fuehrer,
Beneath the ruins of a blind rage?

But, within sight of safety, shouts
And shots ended the dud adventure,
As fifteen partisans, out fishing
In troubled waters, struck it lucky,
Landing without effort or difficulty
The biggest fish of the whole catch.
Il Duce! they yelled, as the bells
Preached revenge among the cypresses,
Promising a pardon to whoever kills.

The place was Dongo. It was a gutter
Killing, in which he had no chance
To strut about, to preserve his image,
Like Bonaparte on the Bellerophon.
They hanged him with a rope of jeers,
Then left him dangling. How a man
Dies, strung up or crucified, won't
Matter all that much. Whether guilty
Or innocent, only our legends count.

Shooting stars in Sicily

The mosaics, *Christ Pantocrator*
Were reminiscent of, though better than
A technicolor film.

Two punctures and a brakesblock
Melted in heat, I limp through the insect
Humming hush, gaining at dusk
The Temple of Segesta.

       Goethe that stage-coach
Did this in comparative comfort.
Valery opines of columns in general:
"They march in time". From Lampedusa
A cynical aside.

Featureless hills. A village
You squint to see, there Garibaldi fought
Overlooks the valley.
       I lean my property
Against a column, then between two columns
Doze, pricked by thistles, facing
The sky. Later the polecats howl.

       Calatafimi
Is probably Mafia-cowed, that bonfire
Mafia-lit. But, somehow, adventure
Does not materialise. This is not quite it.

Only the shooting stars.
The night became less unimpeachable.
More warm and raddled. Stars

As if the columns were flying
Head for Malta; a batch vanishes;
One, slower, flourishes its cloak
Leisurely. Always
Around, they always will be

The Bomb permitting
Chaotic dazzlement, like a Picasso!
Always similes – one aims straight
At the temple, I struggle
From my sleeping-bag and watch till dawn.

Follow, follow
You can't follow. The trajectory declines.
A vulnerability on the edge of truth.

John Wesley visits tinners

Then Wesley left the cloud-sea of the moors,
descended from the crushed sand of the tracks
oblivious to the strident mile-long cries
that poured down from the trenches, as the men
hurled down the rubble-gravel of their oaths
across the viscous landscape. On he strode,
his head filled with the banks of unblown tin,
the black slag of unseparated pearls
thrown down beside the furnace, where the troughs
lay broken by the flat cracked-bottomed moulds
demolished by their ingots. On he splashed,
advancing through the black spit of the rain,
that swilled in through the windholes plugged with rags,
and poured across the saturated floors
washed over by the dungpits, where the child
lay sucking at the dry flap of the breast
beneath the fetid sacking. On he pressed,
his eyes blurred with the damp smoke of the lodes
that plunged down like a black nerve through the hills,
stagnating suffocation, as his lungs
sucked air across the clavels of his lips
and fanned the glowing charcoal of his texts,
their hot wrath like a blowing-shed of fire
that rained down from the red wind of the night
its particles of white and molten ore.

Gardening

I
Most of the time it's enough
That a green tip shows,
Confirming you in the freedom to see
The flowering due next year.
Even the bare patch undug,
Could be feeding
Slow lily bulbs
You gave up for dead.
If buds appear
Be alert, lest you're looking the other way
When anticipation, met or surpassed,
Becomes void for an hour, a day,
For a whole week.
Novelties are not new,
Unless it was bird, wind
That brought the seed;
And finally
You may cease to mind
Whether of currant, yew,
The neighbour's columbine
Or common weed –
As long as it grows.
Nothing's unique
But sunbeam's, light's play
On leafage foreknown.
That keeps you working, eating –
That and the need
For what you think you are bored by:
For continuity,
A place of your own
Where bird, wind passes through.

II
Ripeness is all; but
The apples and pears that last
Take longest to ripen.
This early pear
Turns mushy or mealy one day
After it's ripe.
And the earliest fruit to ripen
Are those with a maggot
At work in the core.

To be slow,to take time,
And what the sun has to give,
Not to fall
In late summer or autumn gale,
Ripening, that's all.

A cornered freedom

Across the soft green risings of the heath
A tide of wind runs in from the icy north,
Eddying through trees, invading the air.
Though by the wilder gods, yet even here
We can't be sure the ghosts of the untamed
Do not come. Though the green ease lulls,
With the wind and the inheld sap-thrust,
Panic as the blood in lust, they come.

Today I feel it, walking under the clouds –
The beat of the earth, a cornered freedom
That the city slowly closes in upon.
With summer revelling in its wintry silences,
The wind's reversal brings the speechless back,
The cityless maurauding vigour
Of the harsh space rulers, for a moment
Breaking all the bye-laws of this civic air.

Deceit in the park

The reason why the Park is closed
To All Persons from nine p.m.

Because persons might discover
There is no mansion there. Because
Someone might just hide and challenge
The uniformed men, unmasking
Apparent bandsmen and keepers.

There is endless garden and no house.
Paths lead only to other paths.
Thousands eat their miraculous
Picnics and roam in the sunshine
Of admission and audience.

By nine p.m. lovers have left.
Dogs on elastic go sideways
Over the turf, nosey but too
Animal to smell out reasons.
The late stroller wonders why
Ordinary trees have names like
Library books chained on display.

All Persons are locked out because
Someone might discover the truth.
Apparent bandsmen and keepers
Have done away with the mansion,
Constructed fanfares and flowers
Where the original sun
Struck a thousand admired windows.

The angel

I am the angel.
I am larger than a cathedral,
Less obtrusive than a bookmark.
I sit in the Resurrection cave,
A radiant figure in repose
At whose smiling sightlessness
And curious sunflower's face
The rough and ready Eastercomers gape.

We are the completion you long for,
Your tears are for our mystery.
We are the prints above the snowline,
The music on an empty ocean.
In every place panicking devils
Find our occupation. In the sea
Where the headlong herd blaspheme
We are mediterranean, baptismal.
In the sevenfold lunatic's head
We keep watch and bless his errors.

Going into the world of men
For Tobias or for Mary,
My fellows are touched with pity
As they think down through creation
Past obedient planets and suns,
To find in the darkness outside Eden
Laborious craft out on voyages
Discovering all the dead stars,
Creation's rejected prototypes.
Instinctively my fellows pick
Meteorites from the path of flight,
As they would dash stones from Christ's feet
Or make to catch him in mid-air.
It is the habit of protection.

I am the angel.
I am apparent in your blink,
At the end of a passage and
Then not there, on the far wall and
Vanished when you look again.
In such imperceptible visions,
At such immeasurable moments
We occur in your mortality.
Mostly we are engaged timelessly.

Thus I sit above the empty wraps
In the cool tomb. The outside
Is to me a blur of grass and sky.
I am here always. When the opening
Darkens and stooping men peer in
I am ready to speak to them.
But their eyes are unused to the gloom,
And often they do not see me.
I understand.
I am the angel
Who was blinded at the Resurrection.

Children's hour

The girl and the flowers are pale inseparables.
Abandoned to the blues and dusty yellows,
half-sister to the white
shadow in the window-pane,
she watches the sleek Arapahoes
fight back across a dozen Godless acres.

Endurance

The orchard is lit
on one side by the evening sun.
Its yellows glow.
An odour of leaves and rind pours in.

Hillsides are dealing with last year's scars –
endurance of the just-visible.
Twin children, hair ablaze,
number the lunatic eyes of moon daisies.

It is the true magic.
In the pause between mind and movement
history claims its own.

Storm at night

Noah once, with animals in his Ark
all bellowing for home,
plunged down the desecration of the dark,
chained to the wake of lightning on his keel.
A dove of peace ignited on the foam.

Beneath his hold, invisibly, the Flood
upheld. Drowned arms forgave
the overriding vision of the blood.
Hot in pursuit of the world's end an eel,
trapped under sheets, surrendered to love's grave.

O Judah

Before I was let out
the wailing wall was there.
Brutal acres of despair.
Silence.   No redress.
Jerusalem.   Berlin.

I saw the trap before the pit
fell in on me.   No face.
No lineaments of love to trace.
All mirrors gone. The one
I loved transferred elsewhere.

Lamentation.   Spring.   Thorn.
The lesson of it all
lay in windflowers on the Wall.
Beat upon the burning air.
Always be one to learn.

Goddess transformed

Finally, after 35 minutes of love
When they still hadn't made it
(The day had been long, they were tired)
She got up naked, to wash the sweat and boredom
From her body.
The man, I mean the other man,
The intruder in the house that night,
The gentleman thief, making his sleekway up
To the bathroom landing,
Stopped, stunned, stock still.
There she was, Venus at least,
Rising from the waves, hair
Matted and long, standing there
Before him, Primavera, Primaeval,
Beautiful.
Slowly, wonderingly, he
Stretched out a hand and—
Took her jewels.
Later in his west end pad, his chick by him
The gentleman thief slept,
Twisting the goddesses pearls
Around his fingers, ropes
Encircling his enslaved mind.
Whilst she, remote,
Stripped of her jewels, transformed,
Made unimagined love
To her good-natured, astonished,
And undoubtedly
          Delighted
                    Husband.

Snow in Zambia

was reported for the first time ever.
Zambians were terrified.

But a meteorologist from Z. writes in
disputing the TIMES evidence:
not snow, but hoarfrost, rime.

This could be of considerable comfort – for them to know,
malgré the frigidity,
that one almost-unused word of their vocabulary
should be rightly replaced by another (or two)
even less used.

As Marianne Moore, making the news
hers, must have said,
this rime has reason.

Near Fredericton
(New Brunswick)

Humming-birds in the bergamots, and bees
along the light alliterative limes.
Ferns at the lawn's end fliff, the aspens though
notice the least puff – swish their silver coins
in leafy freshets. Now it's new-mown hay
outscents lawn-clover, limes, as one more load
comes from the far slope (two young hands atop
sunbathing in a shirtless, hot July).
The crunching sweep of a car hardly disturbs
smooth senses – till it's suddenly a skunk.

Nearly caught in bed by The Queen Mum

Clipping yew hedges, the worst job in the garden,
Stripped to the waist, sweating in the hot sun,
Leaf scales sticking to me like ticks,
Dust fouling my eyes and nostrils.
The twigs scratched at my skin, like your fingers
Searching my naked belly, aroused me, and the glad
Dry wreaths of roses everywhere, this year,
Unspoiled good colours, tender in the sun, some perfect.
Weary, I came in to bath, and stripped beside you.
So, without speaking, we both weighed our chances:
Realising everyone was out, I feigned
A need for help, and you came innocent,
Or not so innocent, and then protested.

So, you gazed out of the window, doubtful,
Until your body told you what to do: no,
I'll not tell all, about that hour
You elegant in earrings, me dressed only in scratches,
And how you were so wild you raced me home,
And how, gasping, we laughed, all the way through!

Oh, help! Here comes the Clerk to the Parish Council:
I dive into my clothes – 'just changing after gardening!'
Surprise! A royal Personage visiting the village!
Supposing they had brought Her Majesty round here?

Ah, well – render unto Caesar the things that are Caesar's.
Holding one breast and the curved small of your back
I was a soul in bliss: worshipping the majesty of your body
I would have had to say: here, Madam, like the angels,
I am lost in perpetual contemplation of an infinite glory,
If only for an hour . . .

Two riddles and a proverb

One
Rises snake-charmingly from leafy baskets,
ticks like a robin, spits like a cornered cat,
lish as a squirrel mizzles up trunks of nothing,
snores into sloth, volcanic overhang.
Is eighteenth century, a powdered wig;
any century, a dusty flag;
suddenly pregnant, billowy-mad;
then shapeless, evasive as a squid.
Stretches a sunny dewdrop, paints the wind,
somersaults mid-ocean over its other man;
is prancing djinn and toppling rick,
crowsnest warning, squaw's headache.
Trips in a maze, all ends and bungle,
fades in the fist, (but can smother, strangle).
Elastic metaphor, a visual pun,
may be seen through, reflected on . . .
alive, a thinskinned ghost;
dead, its own solid.

Two
Dozes with one eye open wary as a dog,
is a harum-scarum, dabhand at tig,
can look blue as breadmould, sanguine as the sun,
tipped with the odd copper turn bilious-green.
Flashes to airy opulence, a gold-leafed thistle,
lilts for the fun of it, a belly-muscle;
hides loaded origins (seamy past
and slippery future) wit; instant mist.
Blurts into starry flight, the sudden lyric,
lives with wooden soldiers in a cardboard barracks
(one of whom, grazed, loses his head, blacks out);
can be more than tender in a bedsit.
Seems bright enough, but chews straws like a yokel;
constant, yes, but as swiftly, fickle.
Loves to summarise, dotes on a clean précis,

likes an ending that's snappy, saucy;
whips your coat off slick as sin
and signs the balance: skeleton.

Morning star

dear killer, dear thief
   (of boredom, of blankets) I watch you with
the sun on your strong head, stony
   with sleep, but refreshing into morning
with a gentle breath, your eyes

are so that you do not know
   theft of wind on pear-orchard
in a swirl of petals
   snowily scaling the window.
Shadows flicker on a woman

staunch with sleep, but mortal. Then
   some killer of a morning
shall blow you, with petals,
   to sleep, one day, about the sun
for a long time and all the same

we may number it in minutes. Therefore make me
   hard for gentleness, in what time
we have, and the facts of the case,
   killer of boredom, thief of the morning
star asleep in the sun.

Weatherclock

a clean and smooth hill
is gathered into a windmill.
under the glass the sails
throw out beams of light.

away round they go, backing
with the shift of the wind.
blue clouds keep their level
in dark still lines.

down on the green by the well
a man with white shirt plain as paper
bends and straightens, while side by side
his pale fists turn the winch.

one way he winds, and then the other,
making the rope quiver.
the bucket reaches neither parapet
nor (by his ease) water.

I am watching and weighing.
I have compassed his trick.
I have not shown myself
and need not speak.

the glass is beginning to fall.
I shall smoothe
my hair, my pinafore
to the door.

The years

Intimate memoranda, your touch
lingering with me, glimpse
of a sunlit lawn long ago,
vestigial presences. How do lives
ever connect? But gently, beyond
years, distances. Nothing between us,
only the clasp of your hand
undermining my silence.

Little Langdale
(*to Richard Holmes*)

Swans on the tarn
move with the weather,
rain, wind or sun,
drifting together.

Evening: cross over
the mountain ridge,
down by the river
to the slate bridge,

up to the stone
cottage. We play
cards, and fortune
smiles on us equally.

I would like words to be
clean as this life,
free as the water,
strong as the earth.

Clocks tick differently

Gary, when they pressed you under,
Did you see the holes in the hands?
Or did the sea water, scrambling
Into your mouth, turn into wine?

Clocks tick differently.
Remember a house, when
The clean book, in the grimy palm, was too obvious.
The thorns, in the distance, could not hurt us.

The calendar, that once announced pressed January,
Opened tempting doors (opened),
Flamed month-marked candles in our hearts,
now crows a creased December and
Closes ajar doors (closes);
The flames?
Yours is the light, of a campfire, shivering
Across the faces of prophets discussing the
Introduction of Mary to Jesus the Christ.
Mine is a smoking, shrivelled bootlace in
The greased face gathered like sharp snowballs
Of discarded words.

Clocks tick differently.
Am I trying to shake rocks through a sieve?
My faith, in a glass case, grows cobwebs!

Fables

I

The gentleman that my black hen lays eggs for
Has diamond links joining impeccable cuffs
And a suit and a voice and a smile of exquisite finish,
But has never been known to express a liking for eggs –
Which is all that my black hen can lay for him.

II

The butterfly is dainty flippant fragile
Like the petal it lands on without moving, while
Man is strong, and marvellous in conquest.

Butterflies cross oceans without fuss
Flitting over arid waters; for us
Even to say 'alas' we need trumpets.

III

This nut withering on the shelf
Enfolds leaves which could contain
Lithe branches, home for singing birds;
Breezes blowing aloft, moist root.

It blackens like an old man's face.
Oh where is the soil and the sweet water
To ease from the crippling shell the shoot?

This small withered nut my brain.

IV

To achieve knowledge, salting away Faust's stock,
Is that better than a certain sort of look
Attained to make another's hackles rise?

Except that the body dies, the body dies.

V

The boy planted a bean
Plunging his whole hand with it into the earth
Which he was young enough almost to want to eat.
His mother, engrossed with the years, lolled by the shed
Getting out the washing in a practised slovenly way.
The boy dug deep, like his father, and the bean grew,
Planted for his loud-mouthed mother as his father did.
In the water-green leaves' reflection the child and the woman
Laughed in their fecund world
His shadow contained within her larger darkness.
Incredible that this shadow of his mother
Will soon be a lean man gobbling up fat women.

VI

A man paid 110,000 guineas for Van Gogh's mother
Not for the woman that breathed, but a picture of her.
If he'd met her when she was what she was
I don't suppose he'd have given as much to her.

And if he had chanced to meet him, would he have felt like
    supplying
The painter, even with enough sausage for the rest of his
    natural?
He probably wouldn't have wanted him in his house:
An ordinary functioning man, sleeping and glaring about him.

And although he has to pretend to value her
Saying he'd give his eye teeth or at least his worldly wealth to
    save her,
I daresay he wouldn't really have wanted to give all that money
To have his own mother sitting permanently on his sofa.

A dog would rather have another dog
Than a flat board,

And is just a dog.

VII
The two young men were warned
They had been told
The blue lagoon was treacherous, that beneath
Its picture–postcard surface lay quicksands.

The frame of bright green trees rises steeply
From water that they longed to flail their arms in
The unscarred strip of silver sand looked firm.

The wood keeps off the noise from the road above:
Their muffled cries were held within that rim.

Visiting children were told this as a lesson
But they became heroes we dreamt we would have saved
Had we been there. But except in dreams
We never would have gone in the wood even
That circled harmlessly, in case some Thing
Caught us and dragged us to the Blue Lagoon.

But later much more arrogant than this
Not satisfied with having what we know
Can never be more safely ours we must

Pitch ourselves in. When dragging currents take us
What comfort to the bodies as they drown
To say to the water spiders 'We were told so'?

VIII
A great bird is swooping over our yard.
Let her have the chickens while she's mine.
We will do without eggs for many a long day.
Looking into the light to see what bird,
She throws blindness like a rage in my eyes.
On all the air, now black, outline of wings
Is clamped like a sizzling horseshoe, like Mercury
Running into itself wherever I look –
The dark fire that neither heats nor lightens.

IX

Stay close, little tortoise, dig in.
Put on the coffee pot fourteen times a day,
Day and night intermingled with much slow pottering.
Put your nose out rarely
So that in the Spring
There will be someone calm to note the spot
Where my beautiful friend the hare
Died galloping across the frozen hills.
Stay close, little tortoise, stay alive
Collect your strength, drip, drip, through months, in a phial
To sing a dirge for our beautiful friend the hare.

X

Fifty thousand cats cross our garden.
No, of course not so many, but a quantity you can't count.
They are gross and dirty scavengers and disturb the night like
    babies.
What weather is brewing away in those foreign skies?
For suddenly looking at me through the window
Is this long-haired fluffy grey tiny cat never before
Seen, gazing at me out of a white ruff.
A prize cat, no doubt, strayed in our mongrel yard.
She gazes sweetly and turns, unsure, away.

XI

Think of the minute amount a mouse eats.
The sticky handles of knives will keep them going
Or the bits of grit from a crack in a biscuit.
Really he takes nothing from you.
Insects build colonies from the side of jars
Where the jam has dripped and dried.
Many people think they only take
Things not used up or needed by rightful owners.
What is one smile a week and a kindly thought?
But think what inroads and depradations
A mouse can make. He can gnaw through a wall in a week.

In the end he uses up everything
One ruinous mouthful out of twenty precious books.
He renews his nestful of needs every five weeks.
Think of the eyeless citadels of the ants
Growing as high as trees where no tree grows.
All will be taken after that first nibble.

XII
The washing is jerked from shade into the sun
And the rope half-hitched round the cleat in the same swift
    movement.
In the well of the yard stands a woman whose huge haunches
Swivel on solid pillars. Her feet do not move.
Her hands can reach to everything she needs.
A band of sun paints the air by the third floor windows.
She has hoisted the dancing socks from dark to light

O woman, could you haul me to grace with your strong right
    arm?

Woods
(*for Phil*)

Through trees down to the road, then up
To the single tree where the dog lay
In shade there, then to the darker wood
With no grass underfoot, a place
For flowering shrubs in summer, reaches
Leading to light, to further woods and then
To the long brilliance of the lake.
I never went that way with you.

You lay with cancer in your body.
To the left ferns and then the coarser
Grass, with deer grazing there;
To the right horses on the track,
The rise up to the hill, then over.
We did not go that way. Ahead
The light reaches of the lake, I
Did not go anyway with you.

Ten thousand miles away three nights
You called me down the stairs in dreams
Of childhood fears. They were not you.
Dark reaches of the wood, the light,
And then the darker reaches opening to
The lake, its other light. They cut you open,
Then closed you up again. No way
To end that darkness. Not with you.

Deer grazing to the left, the
Coarser grass. We did not go that way.
After the war you drove me pillion once
Upon your motor bike. We went
No way I knew for thirty minutes only.
Your screams at night would wake me then.
You said they were not you. They were
A darkness that the war had set in you.

What is it in our lives that opens all
These reaches for us, through the woods
To light, the horses up the rise, the
Coarse grass to the left, the further woods,
Promise of light that opens through them,
Then the lake? I went no way with you.
Then you lay dying; you called me down
The stairs three nights, It was not you.

And thirty minutes on your bike is all,
And no way that I knew. Call me then:
The path down to the road, then up
And to the single tree, the shade, the
Far reaches of the wood, the light
Of summer, the brilliance of the lake.
We will not go. The deer will graze
Among the coarser grass: the horses will ride by.

But call me then, although we will not go.
I went no way with you, and now
You open reaches for me, darkness
And then the light, more reaches of
The woods back from the lake. There is
A shade there, there is shade, a
Single tree. I have no way to go
With you now, We shall sit down there.

Lanes
(*for Randall*)

The bus stop named after the objectionable
Pub just after the turning. You preferred it to the
Thatched piece of Real England in the village.
It was the way you thought things were perhaps;
Hard-lined, cold, unlike you, a place where
One had no place.

Then down the lane,
The mad ice cream van roaring by
In a landscape I could not like. Bleaker
That next winter in a darkness that
Pressed on the eyes. I was a city child;
I had never known it, You dropped down dead
In a London street.
Then down the lane
To the cottage, the dog in summer
Still with his nose in the fireplace. He
Was going blind, laying with his nose
Almost in the flames next winter. The
Darkness pressed on the eyes. I had
No place there.
You could cross
The fields, damp earth even in dry
Summer, to the road. I crossed them
With famous A.R. (dead also now) and your
Daughter. They talked of friendship. 'I suppose,
Young man, you have no friends.' I suppose
That he was right there.
You could cross
The fields five miles to the Grammar School.
It took me hours and the view was nothing.
This was Real England; plovers gone over
Cold, bleak fields, frost behind hedges, heavy
Clogged meals, a choking stove; dark
Pressed on the eyes.
Then down the lane,
The dog going blind but starting up
Partridges he could not catch; and just
As well with the Game Laws, Real England
Still there in the lane, one day in
Hunting pink on a tired horse: I liked that
Being a city child.

                    I would cross
The fields back from the school at one.
You were off to the pub then, down the lane.
The dog startled partridges it did not catch.
Dropped dead in a London street, but that
Was not you Randall, and not your truth
That I would never know.
                    Down the lane
To the cottage. You stood on the hearth
More full of life: dropped dead in a street;
The darkness pressed on the eyes, the fields
Damp even in dry summer, the earth clinging,
Plovers gone over bleak fields, frost white
Behind black hedgerows.
                    Then down the lane,
There is the garden, and the door is open.
You stood there. What was it that was in you?
You read my poems and they sounded truly
Empty, as perhaps they were. Partridges
Startled and not caught, an image now for
Me, but not for you.
                    I cross the fields,
Darkness pressed on the eyes, the earth clinging.
Too many lanes to go down now to find you,
Knowing your death so many years and turnings
After it was. Let it be summer, deep
Summer for you, light on the fruitful
Fields, earth rich and clinging. Too
Many more lanes to go down now to find you.

Fantoft Stave Church

There, against the snow-dark sky
You notice the stepped rooftops
First: dark pagoda top, rigid
Pangolin, head and jaws
With dragon tongues thrust out
At you.

The ancient terror precedes
The full view. As I climb,
I re-enact: build again
Roof upon roof
Against the incalculably long weight
Of snow.

Scaly, dark, unawakened lids;
Jacob's ladder ascending as it falls.
Then the wood has the look of growth
Again, more tree than temple,
Brown pine bent down to spring
Into light.

Rustic courtship
(*to Takagi Kyozo*)

Our elderly go-between,
a scrawny widow,
had a running nose,
and a grubby white eyepatch
only half-covered an inflamed eye.

The last snow was melting from the thatch.
Out in the wet yard
the chickens cowered under the broken shed
and the telegraph wires
heavily strung with pearls
were black with flustered birds
migrated too early from the south.

We sat at a table
barely touching
cold western food.
With lowered eyes and guarded smiles
we silently took stock of one another

and liked what we saw.

The order of things

There is a gun
lying locked away
in a drawer
in a condition
of obsessive calm, casting

shadow
a smouldering
blood-stricken blackness
a nightmare of sweating metal.

There is
embalmed in its box
a locked-away suddenness –
germ of a cliff
darkly under one's feet
caving.

Le lapin agile à Bramber Castle

This mound is raised three inches above allegory;
no tower, no tree, no roughness bastion
inhibits here our vision of the sky;
nor do our elbows touch as we lie
in the time-honoured posture of the sculptured dead.
Here at the pivot of our defences we exist:
chapel down, moat long-dry,
guard-room vanished, wall incontinent.

'Mange–t-on les lapins?'
Your question slips
out through the enclosing trees,
and the nervous pips of shadow
playing in the south-west corner
flash up their tails in the dusk. And
do we eat rabbits? A good question,
one I must decline categorically to answer
as I smile at you from inches inside sanity
here where the soil is firm.

A jade-polisher of the Western Han

It took ten years to trim and polish
The thin squares for the left thigh
Of the burial suit of Liu Sheng,
Who ruled the world on his western throne.
Five thousand men were needed to move
Half a hillside, and in the hollow
They laid Liu Sheng to live for ever.
Hundreds died of whips and hunger,
Were trampled into the tons of earth
That others carried caked with blood
Gritty with broken bits of bone,
That Liu Sheng might lie buried
Incorruptibly clad in jade.

While the bones broke of my thousand brothers
I sat in my shop and sang softly:
   Jade is the stone of the gods,
   The stone of the five virtues,
   Nothing surpasses jade.
   It is hard as courage,
   Clear as wisdom,
   Nor will its colour fade.
   Its edge is keen as honesty:
   It will not cut the workman's hand,
   However sharp it is made.
   Polished, it comes smooth as justice.
   Struck, it sings of purity.

So I sang as I cut my squares,
But kept silent on the sixth virtue.
No prince tortures his jade polishers,
For few can cut a clean edge,
And the trained thumb takes years of toil.
So we leave no broken bones on the hills,
No thirsty soil savours our blood.
We sit in our shops and sing of jade,

And praise the prince as we polish his suit,
Sing over and over May he live for ever.

He may live for ever. But when ever is over
He will be dust in his jacket of jade.
In a thousand years they will break his tomb
And my squares of jade will shine like justice
And struck will sing of a pure past.
No-one will know the workman's name
As the keen edges cut their hands.
Liu Sheng I will live longer than you.

O Sapientia

O Wisdom sounded by the mouth of the Most High,
resounding from end to end, to care for all things
strongly and sweetly, come and teach us carefulness.

I
'She's proud,'
said the carpenter.
'Plane 'er more.'
Curls were shaven,
then he stroked
her smoothed side,
now a perfect fit
for closure,
a working door.

'You lead your LCC
into your threeway
saltglaze spigot,'
said the plumber.
He showed his little lad
what earth to scoop out
in the small yard,
set in the sculpture
and made the connection.

I praised
the particular word,
used in the trade.
I praised the lordliness
of men who demanded
a daily lorry load
of clinker
so that tradesmen
should not walk in mud.

I praised exactitude
in a skill.

For the saving word
must be set
in the earth
like a spigot,
patted and humbled
her breadth,
like the door's pride.

II
'I got the Knowledge
on Thursday.' Dear God I thought
not dear old Reg
a goner to the Guru,
that great con,
false righteousness, erasure
of the tender young uncertain
what on earth to do.

I remembered Cath,
how her mind was sharp and bright,
always a good laugh
we had, till she became
bored by troubles,
blank at an idea, desire,
even people's looks and details,
passed with that null beam.

Reg takes a medallion
out of his left breast pocket,
not religious coin,
but heart's delight, a licence
for a cab.
London learnt is skilful pleasure –
back street, cinema, pub, curb,
saving your presence.

The white goose

Remember the white goose in my arms,
A present still. I plucked the long
Flight-feathers, down from the breast,
Finest fuzz from underneath the wings.

I thought of you through the operation
And covered the unmolested head,
The pink eyes that had persisted in
An expression of disappointment.

It was right to hesitate before
I punctured the skin, made incisions
And broached with my reluctant fingers
The chill of its intestines, because

Surviving there, lodged in its tract,
Nudging the bruise of the orifice
Was the last egg. I delivered it
Like clean bone, a seamless cranium.

Much else followed which, for your sake,
I bundled away, burned on the fire
With the head, the feet, the perfect wings.
The goose was ready for the oven.

I would boil the egg for your breakfast,
Conserve for weeks the delicate fats
As in the old days. In the meantime
We dismantled it, limb by limb.

Azaleas
(*for Polly*)

More familiar to me
than wayside plants poets are
supposed to sing of – the bright,
scentless, hot-house blooms with which
we brighten winter in towns.
Pink and white azaleas
you brought me for my birthday!
When I look at them, their leaves
now falling, and the blossoms
fading at the tops of the stems,
I hear the music of *Manon*:
'*Adieu, petite table!*' – theatre
crowded, and audience rapt.
The pleasure of cities! These plants
remind me of what they miss
who shun our rainy streets, and
midnight conversations.

Gone

Giving you up is like
losing a bad habit,
nose-picking, nail-biting,
the dull solace of my
unoccupied moments.
One has to be alert
or an absence pricks one.
Don't wonder what it was
that filled the space between
thinking and thinking.
        Gone.
My day is like a staircase
with one step missing.

Reading Cavafy in translation

He would never have liked me,
A woman who's ample and hopeful and hard-working,
Bothered by sentiment, neither stylish nor austere.
Yet the loveless cadences of his translation
Warm me like an old friend from the capital
Met by chance on a provincial street.
His observations, not witty, are precise.
Like good stones in a jeweller's window
They give out fire.
They are the bounty of a fortunate life.
I understand too that the original contains
A familiar sadness about the civilization
Falling away behind us, and a dry contempt
For our inept love of the present,
That flares sometimes like beacons before Armada.
A clever friend, he'd be amused to see me mourn
The sky's slow clouding over and my loss of the good to come.

Sunrise after sunrise

Sunrise after sunrise we celebrate together,
Him stuck like a flea on the breast of Geia,
Me with my teacup, musing, braw, and old.
We watch the light lick up on the edge of the world,
And cushions of furry crystals opening and exploding,
Curtains falling and torrential sheets opening,
In soundless gales of onward rushing light.
We witness it, my infant boy and I, like
Those clumps of trees outside, dogwood, birch and spruce,
Standing stockstill in the throttling frost.

   I'm inside my head.
   My head is a nut.
   I've a spike through my throat.
   I'm sad as a dog.

I hold the world
A little apart.
I hold it with my foot.
I do not kick it away.

Sunrise after sunrise we celebrate together.
Earlier each day I see
In the hollow the snowfelted pond has shaken
Its pure white O from the dark, and the willow's
Skeleton is creeping and flaming with yellow.
For me and my flea, spring's coming, in February.
These circumspectial dawns will soon be unknown.
In April we'll sleep them out in independent beds.

What'll I turn to then,
When the stifling frost undoes
And the spike in my throat
Lets go?

Of course,
When he cries then it'll still be natural to come
And pleasantly still assume
The blowsy soft insistence of my role,
Hastily padding to serve my pretty flea.
And goodness knows, except for this,
When he's a man and feels his lion years,
He won't remember anything but my love –
Not winter, nor the frost, nor death, nor anything
That wasn't his and mine, put wholly at his whim.

The backroom cripple

To reckon June
By the slant of the shadow,
The slates of the light,
Is his problem, not mine.
A geometrical one, at that.

To recall or smother
The flare when the heart-
Thrust of the crocus
Breaks earth's dark shell
Will not bother

Him now it's a long
Lifeline of winter's he's sat
In the pale backroom beyond
The August dust and the street,
The music of wheels.

Time and the sparrows cheep.
The neighbours are good.
And the vanman calls
Down the hollow horn of the days,
And the man for the pools.

All recognize
An acceptance so flat
And absolute,
Not to be tampered by pity
Could amount to greater

Than all he has lost –
Encounters, the wind in the street,
Music of dusk,
Sun on the stone, the Advent frost
On the roofs. All that.

This is the day
(*for S.L.*)

I
This is the day
when the traffic stops,
all its golden horns
blazing in the circuses
        to please your name

This is the day

II
This is the day
when the little flowers
walk to the gates
of the parks, singing
        all their perfumes
        to your neck and bones

This is the day

III
This is the day
when the white polar bears
wash their paws
quietly
        in the zoo
        while you lie sleeping

This is the day

IV
This is the day
when the marmoset,
the creature of evil,
closes his book of blame
        and lets you through
        for all time

This is the day

V
This is the day
when the moon
rises
over the cliff-tops of London
      sweet as a white owl
      to breathe in peace for you

This is the day

VI
This is the day
when the stars
have a rival,
all those jewelled names
      racing in air
      to meet your needs

This is the day

VII
This is the day
when the years open
their boxes,
doves fluttering gently
      over the many facets
      of your future

This is the day

VIII
This is the day
when all your friends
chiming like clocks
speak the same hour,
      one for you
      to live and blossom in

This is the day

IX
This is the day
when the post-cards
drop into the letter-boxes
very softly
       in case you wake
       too soon

This is the day

X
This is the day
when all is well,
exquisite weather
sounding
       through all the funnels
       of the steamers in the Thames

This is the day

XI
This is the day
when nothing needs to be done
except to say
this is the day
       this is the day

This is the day

       March 28th, 1974

W. H. Auden
In Memoriam

Your sudden posting from this mortal garrison
Occurred as you had wished without delay or fuss.
In a city of which you were fond you fell asleep
And morning found you already in the past.
But there are many rooms you continue to inhabit,
Mine among them, beyond my tenancy.
What we, your contemporaries, regret
Is never again to hear the virtuoso voice;
One of the few who understood
Poetry was a profession and a craft.
The books, however, on our shelves ensure
That children will inherit what you so much prized:
A close communion with the gifted dead.

All those who shared your understanding for
The plausible future feel a sense of loss.
You'd given much but much remained to give;
Using your phrase: to civil the mad world,
Which is a commitment of immortal length.

Wizard of words, you had a sense of fun.
The spell you cast lasted throughout my life.
We met in a city divided by a wall,
But death for you will be no barrier.
For me among the many your poetry outlives
The statesman's promises, a dictator's millennium.

You were a Byron of these turbulent years,
Though unromantic, never legendary.
You talked of paradigms but did not preach;
Sinned but your poems were not confessional.

Tears are superfluous when such accomplishment
Survives the body lowered in the grave.

Portrait

He lived alone in rooms and every day
Followed an identical routine.
He rose at seven, bathed and breakfasted,
Sat at his desk, wrote feverishly till noon;

Or rather, like a cormorant to the muse,
Went fishing in her lake for images,
Disgorging his catch upon her paper deck,
A shapeless heap of undigested words.

He shook, till lunch, his wings along the front,
Craned slightly forward in a flabby coat;
Then sat avuncular among the young,
His shabbiness an attribute of age.

Dazed by the wine, he read with half-closed eyes
Only such books his youth had known by heart;
Slept through a poem, dreamed of tireless boys,
Then wrote till five to a surviving friend.

At night, shedding the negligence he wore,
A worldly man, he sauntered through the bars,
Took over conversations, laughed too loud,
Or in the theatre hid an amorous leer.

At home by midnight, sometimes not alone,
He threw away his morning's work and wrote
A passage in his journal, which I've read,
About the weather, the price of drink and boys.

Obsolescence of the carpenter

The one great advantage of plastic
is that it holds no surprises;
nothing can crawl out of the woodwork
at you.
Plastic is clean.
Wood has too many connections
with life.
It actually grew
in some incomprehensible way.
Birds sharpened their beaks on it,
wormish things gorged themselves on it,
squirrel-like creatures clawed at it,
dogs urinated on it,
men cut it down
and cut it up.
It creaks.

Plastic is silent,
born of the vat
and the chemist's note-book.
It wears its bright colours
with a quiet self confidence.
It's strong but it's light.
Supposing Christ had carried a plastic cross,
no trouble,
but then we wouldn't have been able
to get the nails in.
Even the greatest inventions
have their disadvantages.

The moonstone

I will have no more fiction. She is
the moonstone on the bed of the pool,
the transmuting eye in the psyche,
the one drop of dew drowned under air,
the coin in the child's jar, forgotten,
for decades forgotten, but seen now.

I am tired of all these lies. She is
the mouth in the bone cell that eats me,
the botfly that grubs in my vitals,
the ever rain, the wet in the stone,
the architecture's impediment,
the quick smile that will bring the house down.

These are the facts, these only. I am
in charge of my passionate terrors.
I have trawled in her sea-change. I have
extirpated the guilt in the cell.
She is being's bride, and non-being's.
She looks up at me. The night trembles.

I am tired of creation's deceits,
that blood is red, the stars beyond me,
and that my dust is uncountable.
There is only one thing. It is she.
The hermetic eye. I plunge my arm.
into the water. I grip my side.

Dead Serpentine

I watch at the fisherboy's shoulder.
He fishes the Serpentine. Fishes
for nothing. Nothing that I can see.
By the mid-afternoon his keepnet
is empty. My interest has grown lean.
Then he catches a nine-finned green thing
and lets it stand still in green nothing
as if the keepnet too were nothing.

The shore water is greasy. It has
matchsticks in it. Far out are sun-cups
and bronzed people in boats. And if those
bronzed people in boats could row me out
I would escape willingly. But here
like a mother-love silence before it rains
death means little to the fisherboy.

The skin of the shore flakes off and soaks.
The boy is the fish, the fish is dead,
a green banana, a submerged thumb.
He has fallen asleep under the green
like an old man. Tenderness of neck
turns to the tender sun. His dead hair
has clung to his chin. I am the boy.
I too can drown in desired nothing.

Stickleback

Male, pale blue, in quietude –
a bacillus in lymph –

with kidney-glue, a bodkin-skill
among sprig-weedy oddments,

makes his tubular nest. Then woos
his world, polygamist

of the pond : coercive,
vicious in rivalry,

rounding up fish-wives
efficiently, in-and-out of horn-

wort, and with no credentials
but his silvery belly's

phosphor of blood. Later,
as at a fabulous den, takes

custody of a generation,
fry for survival, the family-name.

Salutation to Karl Marx

Between the round municipal flower beds
(chocolate drops sprinkled with hundreds and thousands)
squats Karl Marx as heavy as a dull book,
if a bust can be said to squat, and so I hail him here,
my one co-religionist in this German town.
Well met? Ill met? Let us say – oddly encountered,
in Karl Marx Street, no less; what once might have been
Siegheil of *Judenraus Strasse,** and may be again.
For Fate can make Charlies of us, who now puts us up
with some courtesy. She might cart us off
(having done so, often before). Wherefore, here today,
pulling your metaphorical leg I salute you.
Partly in earnest, seeing the moment is transient.

The civilized Muse

Muse of Translations, good-natured girl,
Never dropping in uninvited at inconvenient hours,
But coming, as prearranged, at a proper time;
And not with lavish gifts, and not with dud presents,
Not with the seemingly fine that turns out fake;
But with something handsome and small, & the more I look at it
The better it seems; better, that is, than the gifts
Brought by that other. O Civilized Muse!
Muse of Translations, you come and sit with me,
With a face unlike my own and of great charm,
And keep me entertained, and never leave like the other,
Who comes with half a story, jabbers, and must be off.

* Jewsout Street

The man who knew the make

I cannot see.
I do not understand
Why
This body no longer lives.

I cannot remember.
Yes, clearer now
I do remember.

I remember the day the mill broke down.
I remember the feel of the air,
The very colour of the light,
That day the engine died.

Ever with us in our workplace
Made the ground beneath us thrill
No matter where or what the season,
That engine bound us to its will.

But then, that day, at first a falter
Then a most peculiar cry
The engine shifted in its halter
The engine slowed, began to die.

A vital vein in vital clockwork
Pulsed an oily, wasteful stream
A gear seized and pistons welded
Crying out with tortured steam.
The wheel lurched once, spun, jammed then settled
While boilers cooled and metal ticked.

But then they called up first the foreman,
Then the man who knew the make.
Then the craftsmen, then the guildsmen
Then the ground grew thick with skill.
Soon that wheezing, dying engine
Lived and turned and shook at will.

Yes, I remember how they fixed it
Now my mind goes dull with pain.
The feeling, seeing, part of living
Seems to leave, to slip and wane.

Show me please, oh please I beg you
Show me how and where to mend.
Fix this corpse, this solid waxwork
Restore to life my loving friend.

Bring me up no mumbling doctor
With Yes and No and Just Perhaps.
Send away that bloody surgeon
With cut and probe and gouge and hack.

I want right fast that engineering
Oily-handed Lord of Life,
That overalled, certificated,
Metalmaster, Lord of Life.

Drag him from his dusty cavern
Dredge him from that coaly slake.
Find him, pay him, sign and bind him,
Find the man who knows the make.

Guided tour

My pleasure is accessible to all.
A small red bus will bring you under
Tall trees, and Brigit's tower
– DEO SOLI GLORIA, 1875 –
Commands the northern plain, tipped
With the lighthouse at the Point of Ayre.
Notice Bride's mellow bell, the split
Stair-case that climbs steep to belfry.
Here your road begins, swinging alternately
Left and right. Inside a church wall gap
I place sticks for my lameness: every year
Here summer valerian nods, and winter heliotrope
Spices the January air. The road continues
Notably smooth and modernised. Geese gangle
Across rounded pastures; hawks hover
Above prosperous sheep; sycamores flourish
Over a lone slate gable-end. You are down now
To a thatched tholtan (last station of a two-room railcoach)
At brink of marsh, yielding it reeds for roofing.
A rising bend takes you past two farms
Gateposted with guns salved before 1800
From a French man o' war. Do you smell the sea?
You soon will. Dove Copse is on your right
Where up to forty birds will preen themselves.
Ignore the straight road to the lighthouse:
Cut to the sea, to Cranstal's shifting shore;
Pass the wallstone carved '1855, W.L.';
Wonder, I beg you, at men's constant shifts
Before you sift the glacial debris:
Two seals will marvel as you search for gems.

As if in Springtime

As if in Springtime the woman
is in blossom, white and almost
innocent. Her house moves

from its Euclidean structures
into a different but co-existent zone:
a night-park, where she is loved

by men (three or four that I know of;
there may be others). Through the hours
the house is inhabited by the mating-songs

of birds, but hushed, toned down
to the flat table of small conversation.
In the brief moments she is alone, I think she cries.

Rich burial

I am the king, liquid and solid, set
For ever as you find me, sealed with gold
At every orifice.
                          It has no flavour.
Accustomed to reach for flesh, I encounter gold –
My sleeping partner.
                          Pots and urns contain
Bones of my courtiers, jewels of my wives.
The great gold mask ensures me privacy
While from eternity's bare breasts I suck
Dried water – the convenience drink.
                                      Quite so.

Unremitting God – you with the teeth
And mane – I lie between your durable paws –
Keep me, deep in the freezer, ready when wanted
To utter, once and for all, the words of gold,
And fall, at the latter day, back into earth,
Cosy, degradable, re-cycled, clay.

The skomorokh

Ekh, skomorokhi, the ice is breaking,
it's time for us to take the road.
For now the blood is shaking,
too hard and long it's snowed.
It's time to wander near and far
and let the bear see the boyar.

Pack the flutes and psalteries,
roll the cymbals in your cap.
Silver drips from trees,
gold rises with the sap.
We'll knock on their gates with the evening star
and let the bear see the boyar.

On with the goatskin, up with the horn,
up with the – censors are lovely men.
Rich and poor are born,
not made, yes yes, amen.
We'll find out where the true fools are
and let the bear see the boyar.

Dance goat, dance bear, dance skomorokh!
Sing how the governor lost his seat
by sliding on the loch,
and mime the priestly bleat.
We'll jouk the rope and boiling tar
and let the bear eat the boyar.

The spirit of theatre

When they set the ferret down Fred's trousers
and he pushed his head through the fly,
weaving about with his cute little bright snake's eyes,
and the women shrieked, and the men
banged their beer-glasses, and the band
rolled up their sleeves for the next number –
I ordered another round.

When the finale almost but not quite collapsed
in a flurry of waterfalls and cardboard swans,
dissolving castles, two rainbows, a real
sheepdog, and a tenor merging desperately
into massed pipes and drums while the centre
microphone developed an itinerant howl –
I sighed, but sat on.

When the distinguished verse-play unwound for ever
about man's inhumanity to man
and sprayed its glacial pellets of high-grade anguish
over the culturefest, and the shirtfronts were numb
with appreciation and shushed each creaking seat,
while long bleak flashbacks crawled out, froze –
I applauded and left early.

And when I went back up yonder,
there was Shakespeare lying in wait for me.
'The mountebank returns,' he sounded off.
I could place his truculence
and it wasn't just too engaging. I yawned.
I looked at him, but all I said was
'Tongs and bones, William, tongs and bones'.

PETE MORGAN   179

Oil

With our eyes closed, our mouths open –
And our ears stuffed against the storm –
We slept secure enough;
Not knowing what God was sending.

To-day each wave is fringed
With the blue metallic sheen of oil.
Each strand of kelp bleeds blue
Back to the sea
And the footprints of the herring gull
Are edged in red and indigo.
On every pool and a thin skin of blue and yellow
Mirrors a quicksilver sky.

At Boggle Hole
God has been spitting oil.
Thick brown gobs of it
That smell like polish slick the rocks,
discolour sand.

The tide's reach is a trail of death –
Of feather, fin and vertebrae.
The starfish lies, contused and broken,
in smithereens of crab and claw.

There was a time
We would have named this Devil's work
For coming in October; His month
When the brambling stopped
For the club
He laid across that shrub,
The mawk he set inside the fruit.

The Devil no longer holds good. He
Was all in evil then
As God sat favoured in his sky –
Worshipped, feated, all-seeing.

The one has dropped from favour,
So's the other.

We now dismiss the Devil's work –
Set all of that behind us.

The oil's slick on the shore's
An act of God
And the next tide takes away its dead.

This is me on a bus

This is me on a bus.
The canal, black and calm and beautiful,
mirrors neon-dark sizzling with excitement.
Humid air plops beads of blood on my forehead
and clouds fling themselves at everything like karate fists.
I dodge and duck and dodge.

This is me, bespectacled,
buying cafe time in a glass of milk.
A word, a dirty look could turn me
into a lethal broken bottle
sharp and hard and stupidly dangerous.
But I will work the trapeze with a clown's eyes.
Between the revolution of free air
and the smiling faces I reach for
I'll flit and grip and flow and fall and fall.

This is me, brittle,
eyes sunken like meteorites, glittering.
Seaweed and shoots trap my mouth,
fix my jaw to the soil, to the ocean bed.
This is the health-food waitress with cantilevered bosoms
and not her whose sense I need
(she has small and bleeding breasts).

This is me, waiting,
working brain, heart, balls, and all productive worlds,
stirring the soup of my seed,
jerking organic wheels,
baiting the thudding blood,
churning all into maggot-riddled, giggling mud.

This is me. I know what to do.
I have not become an ideogram.

Mental defectives at the Zoo

Incurious in the town of animals
They are herded gently through the autumn blaze
Their feet diverge, their limbs make sudden sprawls
They squint and flinch, hold hands like castaways.

They turn away from the cages, shy and queasy,
Busy with uncertainties of their own.
We others watch them, covertly, uneasy.
Their guardians smile and chat in level tone.

They sit and rest. The fat youth laughs. Some fret.
The pouch-lipped man yields to a childhood passion,
Devouring nuts meant for the marmoset.
A sad girl scans her nails in wary fashion.

Bored with their faultless skill, the looping apes
Drop down inert, and gaze across the crack –
Narrow but fathomless – at human shapes;
And suddenly the girl looks up, stares back.

Eagle and Hummingbird

Demure water, soft summer water,
Its rolling boulders dropped, its carried logs
Cast white as salt upon some resting beach,
I throw my spinners here, those small, beaked suns
Turning through steelheads, cut-throat, and the
Five-pound salmon come from the sea too young
Along the green, deep channel of their instinct.

I stand mid-stream on rock, its roots in water,
Using the air to fly my singing line,
The burning spindle drifting through the river,
The river alders burning in the sun:
United elements, the one forgiving world
In whose veined heart I stand in a blue morning
Beneath the flash of hummingbirds, the smoulder

Of fishing eagles. Water and stone, fire
and reflected fire, the hundred suns
The river's mirror carries under the trees,
Buoyancy of the light birds, all's here,
All, all is here. And my thin line holds now
The lure of the hummingbird, its spinning
Breast, and the hooked voice of the eagle.

Supermarket tins

There were rows of coca cola
on the supermarket stand,
shimmering under white light,
reflecting silver and red.
And perfectly between two tins
(consciously apart)
was framed her arresting face
so dramatically decorated.
Blonded hair parted with a razorsharp edge,
freckles on a structured nose cast along a classic line.
'I'll see you again,'
I heard myself say,
when really I want to feel
to touch, smell, sense and explorate
the mind behind
the body contours, built of clay.
'I feel I know you.'
she replied
standing by the timeless, cylindered tins.
Her body patterns silently dissolved
as this becalmed, oasis moment slid away
and tins in supermarkets became just
supermarket tins.

Eyes

This man has been in the
telephone booth all day long.
This is no way to foster friendship,
it is a hard burden to bear
this waiting around.
So quietly I open the door,
(having first palmed my penknife)
and tap him on the shoulder.
Just a friendly tap mind you
so free from any anger.
His pleasant face swivels round
and with nonchalant ease
I stab the knife
expertly, so expertly
into his left eye.
And that ends his conversation.

Henry James

Henry James, top hat in hand, important, boring,
Walks beautifully down the long corridor
Of the drowned house just off Dungeness
At the turn of the century. It is 3pm probably.
It is without doubt October. The sun decants
Burgundy through high windows. The family portraits
Are thirteen versions of the one face, walking
On the thick trembling stalk of Henry James.
It is a face which looks like the face of a goldfish
Fed full of breadcrumbs and philosophy, superbly
Reconciled to its bowl. The difference
Between Henry James and a goldfish, however,
Is that Henry James has nostrils. Those nostrils observe
An exquisite scent of evil from the library.
Henry James goes beautifully on his way. His step
Is complicated. (He nurses an obscure hurt. It is this
Which kept him from active service in the sex war.)
Listen and you will hear the trickle of his digestive juices –
Our author has lunched, as usual, well –
Above the sweetly unpleasant hum of his imagination.
His shoes make no squeak and he deposits no shadow
To simplify the carpet. Henry James
Turns a corner. Henry
James meets Henry
James. Top hat, etcetera. Henry James
Stops. Henry James stares. Henry James
Lifts a moral finger. 'You again!'
He sighs. 'How can you be so obvious?'
Henry James blushes and Henry James flees and Henry
James goes beautifully on his way, top hat
In hand, important, boring, he walks down
The long etcetera.

The long-ago boy

Sometimes I meet the boy I was. He's the colour
Of lightning. He leads me
Between stoat tracks, smudged
With bright blood, in the snow.
He juggles with snowballs.

That long-ago boy lolls also in a hollow oak
Out of the sleet, and counts dead leaves
Like winnings. Up to his chin he is
In rusty guineas. He'll sniff
The pinesmoke in the candlelight
And the air on the green hill
Glorified with snow.

My long-ago boy has been busy tasting the frost
Spun like candy floss about
The spokes of a buckled bike.
Already he's sucked the icicles
That bristle from the eaves, and licked
The tongues sticking out of milkbottles.

The boy's ribs are bruised
By the bullying northpaw wind.
When he weeps, it's hailstones.
When he laughs, the loch gets gooseflesh.
The sun is bleeding to death in a puddle of slush.
O long-ago boy, let's spit at it. Tonight
We'll claw all the stars down
That dangle from Orion's stupid belt.

The gamekeeper to his Charges

It's no good kaaking at me,
Old pheasant cocks
From the far copse.
I know where you have trodden
Your haarem hens
And they have crept
Into dried grass dens
And laid your burden down
Under warm breast brown,
And the lone vigil kept.
Something to boast about
Maybe;
But I know more of you
Than you of me:
I know your secret paths
And dry dust baths
And territorial tussock
To challenge cock to cock,
Because I watched
Before the summer laid so close
A cover on
Your bawdy goings-on.
Oh! I have got you scotched,
And you can strut and crow at me
From the deep, far tree.
But however much you call
You won't fool me at all.
I'll do the calling in the fall.

Cathedral, Toledo
(*for Reiner Kunze*)

Ochre and grey the hill springs from the plain:
the flying buttresses
like ribs of shipwrecked caravels carrying
the greed of the Catholic Kings
to a new world.

Yet balanced
on slender shafts meeting in the dusk
of soaring pointed arches
something more than lust
for silver or sainthood:
a stirring, perhaps, of a faith.

The faith, incomprehensibly to me,
of *Pietà* and thumbscrew.

Morning at Zweisimmen
(*for K., who shares my addiction
to the mountains*)

In the hills' neckline
surmised more than seen
the gleam of snow

The quiet made real
by distant cow-bells
surefooted on
improbable slopes

Greenness gilded
beyond the promise
of travel posters

The Swiss cross
soundlessly floating
on the haze

Venice: end of season

The gondoliers have stopped
looking like film stars
The tourist guides are
reverting to nature
The façade is folded away
The city is left
to the rats
and human
refuse

Mary Quant's London

Fields of Quant daisies gently shake.
Their metal stems vibrate
around the knees
of jerkin-skirted women
whose Hittite heads seem oiled.
       Once they swayed
       in a wind
       which blew to us across
       two red-dewed centuries
       of poppy-pins.
This daisy-spring will one day, too, recede.
Always the tokens of inscribed loss
eventually wreathe remembrance.
But meanwhile, outside, today
fire-vans still pulse their sapphire storms.
       Upon a geometric day like this
       when sun bisects the houses' angles
       how often did we warm
       to that bright word
       'galactic'.
Spaced in the shining pages of this catalogue
weightless I drift within a pictured world
and dream the gravitational fields
where new-born calves of smoke
blew shimmering from cars
       in glistening photographs, decade-filed.
       But unbaled shadows lengthen
       over the mews-flat water-butts
       where culex larvae turn and flick
       to minute steel-white watch-hand stars
for in the cropped heads of these fashionable waifs
genocide's children cry once more for spring.
In Liberty print I dream them smocked.
Their dateless necks are thin-stem frail

their faces blossom-white
  and every icy word and letter
  in the world
  for them lets fall a light-edged globe
  which slips right down this shining slide of time
  for flower-heads that early closed
while I with writing hands
give back to child-souled giants with the minds of chrisoms
and the deprived in time's entire museum
these year-fields of the eyes of dawn
and our white-summer calico games.

Sun

While you draw
wild flowers, lie beside
the lane with closed eyes.

Hearing, through open
ears, galaxies
of larks enough to

outsing the shrill whine
of low jets we
yell curses at;

the lowing of cattle
at evening milking time.
And seeing, behind shut

eyelids the sun makes
translucent as petals,
a fiery glow I know

could pour in moltenly, burn
out sight in an apocalyptic
last vision, prefer –

to blinding by
no more than fire –
to 'learn to bear

the beams of love';
through living tissue
see sun for more.

Hoot owl

Evolved for silent
killing in the dark,
obeys the nightly
order – murder,
eats
and mourns the dead.

S/C

I carry my need
in a clenched fist,

the stronger the wish
the tighter the grip:

my craving is compressed
into a stony seed

too firm to germinate;
too tough, too tidily round,

too full of its own inner
self, its I, its O.

Mrs Herbert

Was dirty, a real slut wife, everyone agreed.
There were crowds of kids around the door,
Each time we passed, they seemed dirtier and more;
They fought each other for bread and jam, and kicked and peed.

The cottage like a cow-shit blocked the lane;
Otherwise it was open, with larks and telephone wires,
An upland road; but tin cans, smudgy ditchside fires
And broken prams marred for a hundred yards; only a broken
                                                                pane

Caught clean cold March sunlight as we hurried past.
We hardly knew him; like a drone he came and went,
But she was always there in the doorway, leant
On the half door, sagging like a mattress, her vast

Always pregnant belly pressing on the stall;
Cow figure, sow figure, mother of it all.

Visiting Foreign Fellow

I am not used to dining in a gown,
Much of the talk is too technical dull,
My speciality is limiting;
They do not understand. The students loudly sing

Long in the evening; port is very dear,
I find myself uncustomed to the food.
They try to talk, my English is not good.
I am very correct. Solecisms I much fear.

In the Hall I am much perplexed by dining noise.
One holds a conversation in a too quiet voice,
I cannot hear him. I concentrate, I frown;
I lose all my words; he will take me for a fool.

With my books I sit; my eminence drags me down.
I work late: my notebooks are friends;
       lights go out, out in the town.

Misdeeds, etc.

Joking of the world's misdeeds etcetera
He leaned to his friend & wrenched her hair.

The onions burning in the frying pan
Were domestic comestibles not symbols for man.

When the knife had sliced through the
Rings she had wept: smarting microcosms.

The gestures of morning were as random
As uncombed strands after nightmare.

She'd sidestepped the bull, gained the fence
Which gave. He was over with time to spare.

Bull, onions were as much a part of her
As head of hair, tears, presentiment of war.

Sunday Morning Rondel

She plays the piano in her dressing gown
Leaving me in the attic to sleep.
The communion wine will have to keep
And mature. Just say we're out of town.

Red fillet of lamb is sizzling down
Below, where, splayed by an octave leap,
She plays the piano in her dressing gown
Leaving me in the attic to sleep.

Her clothes hang on without a frown
– Unlike cassocks in a furrowed heap
After matins. Having roasted our sheep
We stay attuned. With a snatch of John Brown
She plays the piano in her dressing gown
Leaving me in the attic to sleep.

Seasonal

In the old habit
of white petals
snow begins

settles the rising generation icily
permissive
of the rite fulfilled unseen

this mystery
calls for not faith not witness
only modesty

in sacramental
white concealment
now begins
the killing of the old

then comes
novitiate green.

Beachwalk

Old candid gull
boneful of air and gannet eyed
disgraced the rock
and rubber footed it
along the line of timid shells
on yellow soles

beakful of swearing to admit pursuit
trips on a porous bone
some message which the sea expelled
hops high
and drops
just out of reach.

On a theme of Wesker

help me to understand
why the crocuses at morning
change into chalices,
but by night are missiles
– alert, bristling

i'm talking about jerusalem

we bombard
friends with missiles,
enemies with chalices,
in the name of crocuses;
among arthritic trees,
lurking bushes,
we make believe
that the graveyard is a garden

i'm still talking about jerusalem

the season of the sowing of souls
gives way soon to summer
and from the reticent earth
skulls and skeletons freely blossom
– while we, the displaced hamlets,
mope and soliloquise
among the burgeoning blooms;
from crutches of crocuses
the bees burr forth,
bearing the burial seed

i'm trying to talk about jerusalem

help me at the ant hill
to hold my lip stiff
as ant after straggling ant
is summarily executed;

ants come, go, so matter-of-fact;
multiplied a million millions
their antic euthanasias
would scream to the high hills
– they are already loud
magnified to man's dimensions

i was talking . . . forget it

all these earthbound afternoons
add up to insecticide;
the groaning garden
gives birth to grinning grave-children,
their newness nourished
on corruption;
insects beget insects
but fail to become butterflies
before the bees drone death;
an ant cupped inside a crocus
cries – not about hypocrisy
of opening-closing flowers,
but about jerusalem

A witch

For her bread
from November 14th, 1597
to December 11th,
when she was handed over
to the Mayor of Toul,   2 francs

For meat, butter, salt and fish
eaten by herself and others
during her confinement,   4 francs

Wine for herself and her guards,   13 francs

Inspection of Court Records,
employment of one attorney,
three scribes and the Sergeant-at-Arms,   34 francs

For the judge, twenty francs,
        (a donation from her estate)

Additional expenses
For guarding the said Cathin Joyeuse
(also known as Mayoress Etienne of Toul)
from the date she was sentenced to torture
                until day of same,   3 francs

Incidentals
For the torturer, twenty francs, and five
for the honest citizen who rode to Nancy
to fetch him.

Period three

I stop before the door, compose myself,
Then enter slowly. Certain faces turn
To contemplate my manner or my tie;
A few glance quickly, anxious now to learn
What Wordsworth really meant, and instantly.
I look around for signs of coming storms,
And swiftly launch into the holy life
Of music and of verse and UCCA forms.

The wind is rising: halfway through Book One,
The man's done nothing but apologise
For not quite being Milton; even worse,
His idle boasts and foolish prophecies
Are fossilised in blank and turgid verse.
I answer: and the correspondent breeze
Picks up my notes and elsewhere sets them down.
I gaze into the unwordsworthian trees,

And know, however dimly, I am right
To proffer in this heavy autumn room
The relevance of all those thinking things
To all these thinking people. Through the gloom
Of apathy, a voice speaks, a bell rings;
Outside the open window, others shout.
The half-extinguished visionary light
Abruptly and annoyingly goes out.

So, irritated rather than perplexed,
I gather up my notes; now from behind
A thoughtful voice asks, 'Could I have a word?'
I tell him, 'Yes, of course: what's on your mind?'
And as he speaks I realise he's heard
It all. He's not the brightest of the class,
But he has seen a poem not a text,
And understood, although he may not pass.

I wander down the corridor, my pace
Too evidently lacking urgency;
A colleague says good morning and I stare
Past him into the dark immobile sky –
That loony poet bloke. I need some air,
But steel myself to teach another bunch.
I stop before the door, prepare to face
Another forty minutes before lunch.

Heatwave

Avail yourself of this good dream
Sent from a heat wave
Upright
Without any drag of superfluous shadow.

Dream the women at the well head
Drawing sweet water
For Christ to turn to wine
Or any summer miracle.
Dream the secretaries out of the lunch bar
Lowering their eyes languid
To follow the creases beneath
The buckle of a Christian belt.

See they all wear
Garlands of shadow
Where the tossed hair falls,
Shadow damson dark
Beneath the fall of breasts,
Black fronts of shadow
That murmur life
Falling between the thighs.

The sun erect gives you this dream
Without any drag of superfluous shadow.
Avail yourself of this good dream.

Blinky Pop

An ancient bugle to his lips, he sounds
his charge on spent-up housewives, pounds
their peeling doors in mock heroic rage;
and leaves with flea-pit woollens (greased *potage
de jour* of hawkers' diet), cast-offs trussed
with laddered tights, 'yer ferrous', bleeding rust,
'yer non-ferrous' – copper, brass – that might afford
a 'handful' for journeys into space aboard
the Brown Ale special: his stubble-banked
canal awash to the gills, the skipper tanked
way out past Hangover Bay, Goliath-framed
in Sally Pally reach-me-downs. Untamed,
his right glass eye with marbled hustler's gaze
surveys a world that's ripe for Blinky's *fais ce
que vouldras* – the eye he lost 'lookin' for work' –
and winks. 'Hey, got owt, Missus?' He will talk
at greater length to few. He scours the sheds
of not so law-abiding folk, and beds
(or what's left), carpets, washers, irons, all
the household jetsam stacked in yards, he'll haul
out, slam on the waiting cart, and later break
down into classified armfuls to take
for weighing. Sid, the aggro son, between
trips to and from the Borstal, spits and leans
against the horse to cadge a tab, a *quid
pro quo* for filial service rendered. 'Did
you see owt like it – gan on, bugger off,
yer lazy git!' and Blinky scowls and scoffs.
For forty years he's worked the fairs, the streets,
and swears he's happy. Scorns police and hates
the middle-classes. Prefers the coarse smog-grey
estates to posh suburbs, prefers to stay
among no-hopers, 'Blackies n' Pakis', and
the ghettoes where a bunch of kids'll stand
to shout 'Balloons, Steptoe, balloons!' He gives
them all away to bait the trap, and lives

for chance: still hovers in the rain, a hawk
half-blinded, stooping to scrap. Across the park
where the garbage flowers in concrete beds, his Last
Post hails the Tyne as Blinky mocks our waste.

From the reflections of Mr Glass

White globe of rain, we are caught
In the drenching hair of the comet,

She mutters through the oak-crown, step by step,
Stair by green stair of fretted whispering leaves
Gathering her gowns about her, with their leaf-smell

She drags her wet white skirts across the lake
Into the green hills of oak trees, her wardrobes
Of many forms, many voices

She is never still, man cannot hold her

What if he could, glass-snake, waterfall
That has uttered the same sound since the mountain
Began, many mountains, many falls of water

Gynoecium of water, bursting rain-fruit
Packed with glass seeds, each whispering with its speed,
Harem, I walk to the river's source,
I look up at the clouds

Mr Glass, what do you expect
When you plant the transparent apple-seed?

A glass apple-tree
With crystal fruit.

Bite into it.

Glass juice runs
I am poisoned!
I am complete crystal!

The sun shines within you
Chains of yellow buds, briars;

Angry, you focus it along your arm in rays
That strike where you point, Fulminans!
In the dark you are a waiting seed,
However dark it is, there is enough light
To gather within your darkness like a seed of light

The man who arrests me becomes transparent!
The man who shoots me becomes transparent!
The woman who loves me becomes transparent!

To the known God

Priests! you should not have left conjuring.
It is a healthy, relaxing art.
It is good to move among swarms of magic.

It is good to follow service day by day
And woo the god of that church with ceremonial suppers
With hymns ringing in the stone and blessed water
And see nothing and feel nothing
And pray to the unknown god

But it is also good for one learned in vestments
To visit the bonfire crackling like a released footprint
In the green wood and the quiet persons gathering,
Polished antlers, glowing in the firelight,
Who speak to their priests as equals, some of whom are gods
With straight backs and animal heads

It is good to have one god running the daylight
And another running through the dark on great thews of venison
Who dines on the cooked venison
Who runs with the does made of venison
Who speaks with a venison tongue
Who created venison for his pleasure and yours.

My aunt

In life she was unliked
my no-good Aunt
A Man-eater, they said,
seeing her mud-brown eyes
shift, sinking, shining,
calling
And, in truth, she was a rotten mother
to her children:

Last week
she killed herself
alone
in the Mayfair flat
she could not afford.

When they broke down the door
three hot days later, mid-July
they said her mud-brown eyes
still stared out, glazed and
beckoning
from the rag-doll on the floor
oozing excreta.

Today we all stand
serious and still,
dressed in sweaty dirge black
listening to the red gobbling turkey
intoning words
we do not believe.

I am ashamed
that it is only I who cry
these self-induced tears of fear
when I see the honey-pale
gloss-shone box, with golden rings,
jettison my no-good aunt
and her lecherous eyes
            to the flames.

London Irish

London Irish . . . the infamous London Irish.
A row of them holding the bar up; each one
a caricature of the one before and after.
Concrete on their boots, and brogues thick
and dark as the Guinness they swill like
it's the first or last barrel. Singing
out of tune to an out-of-tune band: 'To see
the sun go down in Galway Bay.' Every second
word an expletive: fuck with two o's. They
call each other by the county they come from:
Mayo, Limerick, Sligo: talk about the 'ould country'
as if it's a million miles away and no hope of
return. Later, they'll clamber over their wives
like spastics; fall asleep with a hand between
her thighs. She'll bite her lip while he snores
and soaks the sheets in beer-sweat: in the
morning will say everything, or nothing.

The pig pink rail

The pig pink rail and the sun
in the silver corner slid,
(Remember the time of roses and remembrance,
of golden rods turned amber?)
and glanced off this great ephemerid.

Didn't we question the eagle,
and hold it by a razor blade?
(Geotropism, o how we dreamt of sparrows!)
All that's left is an old ideal,
hidden in the wake of this great ephemerid.

Then was our chain with Ezekiel,
then were geostatics formed.

Pro and Contra

i
Dark codes the woman,
oblique in her nest of riddles.
OF HOW LIGHT FORMED she speaks,
and goes to rest.

ii
'How jolly,' she said, 'to go out
on a spineless night
with soup and sympathy.'
'How tedious' he thought,
'to go out for the same.'

Emma Howard in Hyde Park

Vulnerable as an astronaut,
with whole new worlds of dust
to taste and scrabble in,
you falter and accelerate.
Somewhere white faces turn
like great cold stars.
You elude a stratosphere
of hands, and handkerchiefs,
trailing your beauty like an old toy.
You are bland as celluloid.
Where you are is you,
a little savage queen
countenancing diplomats
only for the things they bring.
Where you are is you,
Emma, and you are two.

To a dead craftsman

I cleaned your tools today.
They lay in green baize
and along the oak racks
of your chest, the way
forty years of craft had them lie.

No weapon hoard
could be more legendary.
I lift the pale-handled saw
a liner-steward brought,
a long Diston, Pittsburgh forged.

The plane for mortising
bought in your youth, used
just once, the great black plane
I unscrew and grease, a thing
you never would allow me, living.

You knew your peers, were
at the end the last
among them in our town
to turn a wooden stair.
Among the living such small fames endure.

Stamped on a chisel haft a name
'D. John', your own below it.
Defying the anonymity
of craft, hands in time
honour the paler hands beneath them.

My Passover Poem

My Passover poem is a turtledove
resting in milkweed.
My arms are linked in Ted's
          walking on bare swamp
                where birds nest in rusted oil drums
                   and the seagull's young
                      are eaten by cannibal crows.
I wear your serpent cincture
The Juggleur wears one, the Magician
We were bounded by serpents, vegetables in earth
    grown in suburban gardens
Is that why serpent cinctures mean forever?
Your eyes were shaped like copper pennies
Pentacles and moons dissolved our pulse.
Come close. Come close. Your sword cane
has a silver handle. Your voice
is milk smooth. I cannot feel the edges of your tongue.
But I feel you all over.
You were are, are
                are always young.
And I am an old woman housed forever in young flesh.
who cannot grasp your concrete world.
Buildings, steel, vertical, soar beyond my reach.
Steel structures have no seams.
Why do your lady friends put make-up on their faces?
Money is the current issue in all magazines
The boom is now nostalgia
You like me in a dancer's leotard
Perhaps
          you see girls dancing over rocks
Or over clouds
When you fly hours
                into Washington
                   or Rome or Tel Aviv
Believe
      that in the second decan of the Autumn balance

I love you
and my eyes
                    are all snakes leaping into fire.
We
    were born under the same sign
The balance of the scales means to see all things
To pour eternity from vessel into vessel
                                    measured out.

The King of Swords is a dark man
I can. I can
                live in your public world.
Your skin is dark and tawny
        pressed olives in a grove.
Your mind is full of dark orations
Sold to podium persons
whose thoughts come from your mind
Be kind – love – I feel weak and small
I have no recollection of my past
Our racial history fills volumes
Yours is in the anecdote
        filled with a who's who of times
            when my hell was a crowded schoolbus
I thought you should have built an empire
Stacked cards, pyramids of books, trumps for fools to follow
Or did you know that they would simplify, distort.

His thought-fly and widow spider

She hides.

He wakes up happy.

She disguises herself
as a wrinkle.

He goes out and gets drunk
on his own iridescence.

More watchful than a concierge,
she squats in the dark left from last time.

His eye squinting in all directions
his gyroscopes to cock
he clobbers the avalanche stairs with his fly-boots.

She draws a living diagram in sticky ink.

He crumples the thunderous doorknobs –

a single synapse-tickle
clouts her poison to the brain.

Her insides outgrave mineshafts.
They are bottomless des-
ponds.

Dream poem

A simple set-up, really: the long black road
Leading downhill and, sensed rather than seen,
A single lion ready to run in a furrow
Beside the verge. An electric lion, perhaps.

The pace quickens – first mine and then the lion's.
If I run, he runs, and if I choose to affect
A Sunday stroll, he lumbers slackly. I plead
Zeno, and fit my feet together in pinsteps.

At the foot of the hill, three nurses in grey and white
Pose with prams on a terrace. I shout a warning,
Run for a well-placed door and throw myself in.
Three white faces stare after me, blank as steel.

Logic's no good for dreams: it takes more than Zeno
To match a lion with nannies, wildness with control.
But mostly, from such conjunctions of blood and order,
It's the heart, doctor, the ageing heart which suffers.

Away
(*for Charles Hyatt*)

I hold a banyan of memories of home
in my head; I have a Rio Bueno of slides:
an unbroken flow of air mail envelopes,
their zig-zag borders carrying on and on,
until the unseen sender returned and died;
someone else, just as faithful, a Harriet
who stayed beside me but who also died;
a large dining-room blackboard on which
singular verb matched singular subject;
that end-and-beginning-of-year Swift ham,
brown with sugar and jabbed black with cloves;
the slow, slow understanding of '38;
those very painful examination years;
the inconsolable lack of a community bell;
abeng, broken again and again, and discarded;
the lizard on its back; the waste of men;
the long line of women at the bottom of the hill;
the warmth that goes for nothing; the lies;
the story no leader will tell; the drift;
the blaze of poinsettias; the sunset at sunrise;
the burning image of West Kingston as hell.

The voices in my room say something, perhaps
nothing, at all, that really means anything.
And yet, they persist. They claim they have a way
with history, with all the people who make it.
Meanwhile, the everlasting banyan spiders the earth
and slowly penetrating Rio Bueno flows and flows.

Spot-check at fifty

I sit on a hard bench in the park;
The spendthrift sun throws down its gold.
The wind is strong but not too cold;
Daffodils shimmy, jerk and peck.

Two dogs like paper bags are blown
Fast and tumbling across the green;
Far off laborious lorries groan.
I am not lonely, though alone.

I feel quite well. A spot-check on
The body-work and chassis finds
There's not much wrong. No one minds
At fifty going the speed one can.

No gouty twinge in toe; all limbs
Obedient to such mild demands
I make. A hunger-pang reminds
I can indulge most gastric whims.

Ears savour sounds. My eyes can still
Relish this sky and that girl's legs;
My hound of love sits up and begs
For titbits time has failed to stale.

Fifty scored and still I'm in.
I raise my cap to dumb applause,
But as I wave I see, appalled,
The new fast bowler's wicked grin.

Where shall we go?

Waiting for her in the usual bar
He finds she's late again.
Impatience frets at him,
But not the fearful, half-sweet pain he knew
So long ago.

That cherished perturbation is replaced
By styptic irritation
And, under that, a cold
Dark current of dejection moves
That this is so.

There was a time when all her failings were
Delights he marvelled at:
It seemed her clumsiness,
Forgetfulness and wild non-sequiturs
Could never grow

Wearisome, nor would he ever tire
Of doting on those small
Blemishes that proved
Her beauty as the blackbird's gloss affirms
The bridal snow.

The clock above the bar records her theft
Of time he cannot spare;
Then suddenly she's here.
He stands to welcome and accuse her with
A grey 'Hello'.

And sees, for one sly instant, in her eyes
His own aggrieved dislike
Wince back at him before
Her smile draws blinds. 'Sorry I'm late', she says.
'Where shall we go?'

Jenny in darkness

She's been in that room for seven weeks
won't go out.
I breathe in old air. Here below the pavement
She's sinking into forgotten shadows.
Eyes shining. Lips tulip red. Odd grey corners.

You look well.
Got any cigarettes.

In the white square
star-shaped blossoms cracking open.
Down here you're without light.

I've given up programming
Don't send me anyone from the Women's Movement.
My marriage continues. It's indestructible
But I'm working on that.
Who's that walking in the next room?
When they're safely dead
I, the inviolate, the uncorrupted
shall emerge into the white light of the empty square.
I dance on a swept pavement under drifting faces –
I leap and the white light shivers into poisoned threads –
I cry and the ruined air cries back the plain statement of a
                                        final solution –
you see, as the borough recedes, I become real.

Outside, rush-hour up Sloane Street.

Encounter

I've got three folding chairs. Ordinary chat.
Burning behind my eyes. You may cry, you said.
You can do it. Your small hands
almost too soft for bone, felt for my neck.
From between my shoulders
warmth spread. "I am a man, but I may hold you."
"It is not forbidden." The gold hairs on your arms
were a scent of sunlight. In your old room
your arms came round me. Through your dilated pupils
your heart stared. Sadness muttered in our faces.
Your room was soft, like the inside of a human heart.
Trees held it above the earth.
You gave me warmth. I wanted to be nowhere else.

By your breathing walls – such quietness.
Behind your sad face the beating of your clear heart.
Silently my hands fall on your warm palms.

The secret

The wagtail's semaphore in black and white,
A diadem spider, tense on corded dew,
Globular clusters of slow snails, clambering
     At the wall's foot:
The daylight, filled with speaking likenesses.

Yet the dusk found him clenched, all lost for words;
The landing clock, hummocked by shadow, knew it.
Then a blue print frock, loose and talkative,
     Spilled, interposed.
The conversation hung by a friendly thread.

She turned. 'Is anything the matter?' 'No.'
Only the fluttering secret a child must keep
Safe for the cold white acreage of sheets,
     The moon's barred face:
Cows in the dusk, floating their clouded tongues.

Rain, sibilant on grass, came troubling on.
At night, while the old house cracked its joints
Or shivered its dusty timbers, the fledgling secret
     Broke out its wings.
When morning sun glanced in, his bird was flown.

Confusion
(*Some reflections on the fate of the Music Hall and other landmarks of Aberdeen*)

THEY have taken away my habitation,
They have taken my town;
I am an old man little regarded
But my grandfather subscribed to the Art Gallery.

They have made a study called Gerontology
In which they show that the elderly become
    confused
When the ornaments on the mantelpiece are removed,
So how do you think I feel
When they take away the Kirkgates
Upper and Lower. It's like losing your teeth.
My grandfather who died with every tooth in his
    head
Cleaned them every day with salt and water
And subscribed to the building of the Art Gallery.

When I was young
And when I was young till I was sixty
You could go back after ten years
And everything would be the same;
The flowers in Strawberry Bank
The smell of the New Market
The number of raisins in Kennaway's London buns
And the old stone houses in the Gallowgate.

I am diminished when you take my past.

Every time I walk along a street my grandfather
    walked
And go into a shop in which all my aunties
Aired themselves and their most doubtful
    pedigrees
I am enlarged, I am sustained.

They tell me they are going to do City Centre
   Renewal:
But they can keep their Walkway,
   keep their Complex.
I have my walkway in Belmont and Back Wynd
And down the Market Steps I had my Complex
– Small stone curves on the window tops
And the great roaring curve of the New Market.
When my grandfather had a drop in on a Friday
He'd walk across the babbling gossip of the Green
And stretch his arms about the walls and cry
"Now here is the bravest backside in Aberdeen."

His affection for the Music Hall was more
   respectful;
Sober he'd lead me in and tell me
" The gentry had their parties here and now its ours,
Ours is the double cube, the round, the square –
Of course it's shabby. Just you wait
We'll have a Socialist Town Council yet
With money to conserve our heritage."
Hush Grandfather, I said, and hush he did,
To watch a woman dressed in white
Pretending to be a swan.

"When you are old you can say you saw her."

It's true I saw Pavlova and now that I am old
Wait to see waterclosets in the Round Room
Dispersed amid the Corinthian white and gold.

I am an old man little regarded
With no teeth in my head
I seek my dear familiars in stone,
The friends who comforted my youth being dead.

Joe the shepherd

Joe once told me the one sure way
to get a champion sheepdog.
"Take a few puppies and starve them,
then one day go and beat them hard.
The one that snarls at you you keep,
the rest you can club on the head."
His words came back to me that day
I watched him at the Yorkshire Show.
Old Joe before the cameras,
with a happy dog lover's smile,
patting his champion sheepdog.

Minipomes

Happening to pass a Roman Catholic church,
He stops and gazes,
And has the sudden thought: if they are right,
I'm wrong to blazes.

I do like to be beside the seaside,
I do like to be beside the sea,
It must be because I'm,
Sprung from protozoic slime
Beside the seaside,
Beside the sea.

To cease upon the midnight with no pain;
Delicately phrased; not likely to corrupt us;
But doubtless Keats, with Fanny on the brain,
Imagined a *coitus interruptus*.

Seascape

Always those beautiful girls;
Figureheads at the prow,
Taking a turn at the helm,
Coiling a rope at the stern;
Slim against the skyline
In Neptune-seducing slacks.
Where do they all come from?
The cabin-cruiser itself –
Twenty-thousand pounds if a penny –
That's easy enough,
Simply a question of money.
But the girls?

Ah, yes.
I expect you're right.

Some usual remarks about the weather

Blue Morning
In the blue morning,
dreams with no trace of decay.
I am eating strawberries.
You look at my red fingers
and smile at the stains on my white skirt.

Water Gardens
The gardens move towards flowering.
You speak of waters: fountains, rivers, oceans.
I am silent amid the odours of leaves,
I taste the weather-edge of rain,
inklings of storm.

Shadow Orchard
In the orchard,
there are no shipwrecks, no debtors.
We walk from shadow to shadow.
Here there are no disputes.
Silence forks, like love.

In the seagreen woods
In the seagreen woods
we stretch summer out to its full length.
By the waterfall
we see all the rainbows:
they astonish us and all Europe.

Cat

1
Mister Bones, Mister Bones:
what must I make for you?

2
You should come back, food is laid,
and milk. You are a black
sombre cat.

        You glower
and are mild. Your cry – its calculating
delicate balance of abandon connects.

I lift you up, and hold you;
a fang of milk, at the jaw,
whitens white hairs. Is one
paw broken?

All your excellence has left you
it has not left you.

Like a black leaf.
The pavement steps over you.

        And the new man
of England steers the hot car,
whose grave power makes straight
the road's maythorned or grimed bends.
Seated by him, his woman's
moist basis transfigures;

each ounce of your black sweetness
is illicit; the road's car

        is prime,
elate steel,
side-haired, cravatted,

a damp organ;

the airy demeanour of it.

Air fragments
and wastes its silence
of splintered rhythms.

Your teeth biting
into death. We had to prise
them open, and there,
a little drench of blood
between your tongue and palate.

Cat. Cat. Your head familiar,
stiff, and animal

I want to hold you, for a long time,
to me

You are amply with us
your pelt, a dark intestate ghost
slim, wailing

in any form, bring yourself
free of the wheels

Robinson Crusoe

Before I left the island
    that book was in my head –
people must see you
    or you must tell people.
Man Friday hardly understood
    a word I said.
He just walked in one day
    and helped me lay the table.

He seemed to worship me
    or my gun or my strange ways,
but would get suddenly bored:
    he might have slit my throat.
We understood nothing together.
    He would disappear for days
and then come back, grinning,
    hanging on my coat.

I will call it love in my book.
    I have a tidy mind.
When the vessel came to my rescue
    he had gone out.
Whatever he thought I was
    I thought he was left behind.
But he fills my dreams. He is inside
    my head hanging about.

Rogation Day: Portrush

I stop to consult my diary and think how queer
that in my day farmers can be sincere
kneeling in stiff suits, their rough hands
joined, praying for swaying cornlands,
a big yield, reward for labour, a reply
from the dumb planets and the gaseous sky.

Upstairs my hands grip the shoulders
of a kindly lady. Between the unholy boulders
of her thighs I play Moses with my loins.
Below, when the spinning disc stops, coins
flow in *Sportsland*. One has picked the right slot
in the one-armed bandit. I hear the jackpot,

and I ejaculate and the girl-friend sighs.
The farmers stand and rub their eyes
for this is a miracle and all the walls are glass.
They can see through the church and up my ass,
and the boy waging his penny in the one-armed thief.
Lord I am lucky: help thou their unbelief.

Replay

Dead
your face keeps
coming at me.

Pale-faced at the window
you pass endlessly
through and through.

And I'm ransacking
my mind for photos,

trying to change
that last image of you.

For a minute
I have you smiling
in the garden,

then a wedding –
in the sunlight
your hair gleaming red.

Click.

I've lost it
and you're
coming at me again.

Framed forever
in that
iron hospital bed.

The novelist

A recumbent figure:
he realizes the fiction
latent in his loss of hair,
the green bird descending

or his ornate, onyx clock.
"Relevance", he says
with legs outstretched,
"encompasses all".

The match explodes within his pipe,
his cupped hands poised as if thought
resided in the tips of fingers,
and, of a sudden, what is not

is what could be existing
in probability.
Tea with a slice of lemon
shared under a cool and

aluminium sky set down
in scattered typescript.
Long memory is age.
Faces float in recollection;

no imagination
viewed these passively!
Then the theatrical leap
pushing the garden table aside:

"An ado about Isobel Archer!"
The autumn garden harbours his age
reflected by the ivy's red glow.
The late sun hints at rebirth.

Sunlight on the Forth

Sunlicht on the Forth
It's dawn in Fife
By me sleeps she
That holds my life.

I, sleepless, hold but a whisky glass . . .
—Ye silly bugger, hold back t'your lass!

Sunlicht on the firth
The blink o' an ee,
Bleery, bonny,
Says "Come to me".

Sunlicht on the firth
It's dawn in Fife.

Song: She fills the heart

There never was a time I kent
Nor ever a place I lingered lang –
There never was a love I had
   That filled the heart as she does.

Ye gowk, that's what they all tell
Since Solomon strummed his sexy sang –
The lover thinks nae lass that breathes
   Could fill the heart as she does.

They could be richt, auld Dryasdust,
As like indeed they could be wrang –
For me I've never drouned a draught
   To fill the heart as she does.

Ay, fill and owerfill and run
And dart the selkie seas amang –
I'm never like to find a lass
   That fills the heart as she does.

Goodbye to Wilfred Owen
*(killed, while helping his men
bring up duckboards, on the
bank of the Sambre Canal)*

After the hot convulsion, this
cold struggle to break free – from whom?
I am not myself nor are his
hands mine, though once I was at home
with them. Pale hands his mother praised,
nimble at the keyboard, paler
now and still, waiting to be prised
from wood darker for their pallor.

Head down in a blizzard of shrapnel,
before the sun rose we had lost
more than our way. Disembodied
most moves on the goose-fleshed canal,
dispersing slowly like the last
plumed exhalations of the dead.

Four places

Aberdeen
Old daughter with a rich future,
that's blueveined Aberdeen,
reeking of fish, breathing sea air
like atomized pewter. Her clean
gothic ribs rattle protests to the
spiky gusts.   Poor girl.
She's got to marry oil.
Nobody who loves her wants to save her.

Dundee : Night Wind
At sundown, a seaforce that gulls rode or fell through.
The small snow is surf. Eddies of strong air
swarm up old tenements. Listen! My window's
late rat-tat-tat guns back at who and whose enemy
milked the sky's agates, polished its ebony.
Someone's ripped cobwebs from a great dome's rafters,
revealing a moon-face, a star-field,
barbarian Orion crucified in God's heaven.

Oxford : By the Boat House
They belong here in their own quenched country.
I had forgotten nice women could be so nice,
smiling beside large sons on the make-shift quay,
frail, behind pale faces and hurt eyes.

Their husbands are plainly superior, with them, without them.
Their boys wear privilege like clear inheritance, easily.
(Now a swan's neck couples with its own reflection,
making in the simple water a perfect 3.)

The punts seem resigned to an unexciting mooring.
But the women? It's hard to tell. Do their fine grey hairs
and filament lips approve or disdain the loving
that living alone or else lonely in pairs impairs?

Mallaig in Spring Sunlight
Reach Mallaig and experience the same thrill
you'd feel if you died and discovered
Heaven was real. Herring stir
the harbour into haloes of seagulls, or else
birds in free, dissonant chorus are
themselves white angels.

The ships glide in gracefully, like souls
assured of their salvation, not pretty
but exclusive and competent.

A work-a-day place. We should have known it.
How could we have imagined it other
than as home for the unimpeded,
the locality of accomplishment?

The fish, to my son

What eye, obsolete and monstrous, blue,
In blue bath of pupil, beautiful,
Occupies this specially prepared room?
No-one knows you, yet you compel joy.

No one knows you but you compel joy –
Unknown before and hardly discernible,
A joy quite different from happiness,
One that is always present in some form.

How then to address you? For a long white spout
Of want is all the rhetoric you need.
The whale of the blue sea is your eye
And winks at all our dear formalities.

Yet I hold you in my arms, may kiss or crush;
I come upon you basking on a rock,
Strange and rhythmic, mermaid, mythical.
I touch, hold, grasp and am vanquished by you.

We smile within our bellies, but you laugh
With the sudden wind that rattles at our doors.
O such infinite care propels us here,
To hold you, feed you, sing to you, and grow old.

Justitia

1

I never thought we'd need her here,
the Arch Deaconess Justitia,
who seemed conspiratorially always
on holiday. The sky was pink or blue,
the sun burst blind down on alley
without the jostling of factions or the weighing
of the little silver scales.
She came with the rain and evaporated
with the passing cloud; words stood alone
and the language was love, was lyric.
She never showed her face at church
nor among the pigeons at eventide.

Rather in the lifting of a brush
and its application did one suddenly
seem to stand, stern and reproving
as Giotto painted her – somebody's mother.

2

This one would not stand for 'eventide'
or words like that. She would demand
a clear causality; evidence
of visible objects. No sounds or smells for her –
"Such a thing does not exist." she'd say,
scaling off tapestries, violins and dusks,
and decapitating a straggle of angels.
"Such things are not even dreams", she said.

And eventually she has become right,
because these borrowed tarnished images
intrude less and less into my mind.
Painters created them; those painters are dead
or very old. 'Very old are the trees'
and very old too these fabled realities.

Poem in a strange language

Starlings, the burnable stages of stars,
Fall back to earth, lightly. And stars,
Propulsars of angels, die in a swift burn.
And half the angels have fallen below the horizon.

And, falling like alpha particles,
Re-charge the drowned woman
Floating in the bitter lake,
Her hair gold as their blood, her face amazed.

She is Lot's wife, her naked body
Sustained by the salt she has loosened from,
And as her eyes open, grain
Turns green-golden on the black earth of Sodom.

I enter your poem, Mandelstam, yours, Anna
Akhmatova, as I enter my love –
Without understanding anything
Except its beauty and law.

And the way its cloud of small
Movements lifts lightly the fruit
Of a painful harvest and moves
With singing vowels away from death.

Poem of the midway

Where shall we meet, Marina
Tsvetayeva? Have you any
suggestions for our rendezvous?
And in what year?
I shall clutch a photo of you,

but what of the breath

rising and falling under your
coat, your flush, your rumpled
hair? (You'll run from the station).
What will you wear?

Somewhere midway. Not in your own
city, Moscow. They stole that
from you. Perhaps in Prague,
the embankment, or the cafe
full of whores and tears
where your love left you –
yes? (I am jealous).

Somewhere midway. Or I
will come further, let's say 1950
(aren't lovers prone to
pathetic rushed decisions!) ten
years beyond your death, twenty
behind me now. And not
any street that is likely to
rob me of your whole
joy: you will kiss

more beautifully than any,
and I will love you so fiercely
the wild nerves of your poems
will translate straight into my tongue.
Dress for me with the tremulous
awareness of the stripped.
(My hand trembles, shaving).

Our small talk through our night
together! (We won't sleep).
I know from your poetry
what you think of God, love,
and your life – that suburb
of a town you're exiled from,

but I want to know your tastes
in wine, clothes, films.

Where shall we meet, Marina
Tsvetayeva? Anywhere in Europe
and our century will be dark
enough for our assignation,
and your poems I'll come holding
will give us enough light
to talk by, across a table.
How cool your hand is.

A Moment in the South

How different the day when the great composer
Arrived with carriages in the white piazza,
Advanced through avenues of oleander
To where his willing host, full-bearded patron
Of ancient lineage, greeted him on the loggia.

This was the place (the genius knew at once)
Where he would set that awkward second act:
A hanging garden under which the gulf
Spanned sun and haze in a long breadth of blue.
Such was his exclamation to the Count.

The tourists' brochure throbs with reverence
At this munificent and thrilling scene,
Enacted among fragrant southern trees,
When in the white piazza old men sat
Watching the dust rise from those carriages.

Stereoscope: 1870

A trick of cinematic archaeology,
A wooden toy to gaze in, among views
Where rigidly the poses now amuse
A casual audience that gasps to see
How three-dimensional such people were,
With different clothes and different hair, but all
Clear in their different rooms as we are. Tall
Men lean on mantelpieces; children stir,
Or seem to stir, restless at nursery tea;
A wife works at her crochet in a chair:
And all live in a world at which we stare
Because we recognize perspective, see
How everything is close or distant, not
Smoothed to the level pages of a book.
It is at that we almost dread to look,
Such depths, such closeness, rooted to the spot.
Peer through these eyepieces: the past goes round
Like mill-sails turning where no breezes blow,
And where we were a hundred years ago
Tugs us as something lost, not to be found,

Or sought elsewhere a hundred years from now.

Gunshots

We drive along the coastal road
lines of surf rolling in
bougainvillaea   deep purple
against the ochre dust of cliffs
the fishing-fleet rocking
beside the Chorrillos wharf.

Walk along the empty beach
hard sand   a skirt of debris
we stop   stoop   examine it
millions of dead snails crabs
reddish shells of *muymuy*
mother-of-pearl mussels
hard red gravelly starfish;
crustaceans and molluscs
we'd not dreamt existed
and guano birds picking, pecking
along the tidal hem.

Out in the bay   silver tuna
with a glint of turquoise
leaping out and flopping back
into the black sea-swell
in their hunger for anchovies
porpoise furrowing across
black fins and dorsal curve.

Some underwater cataclysm
the seabed fractured
the tide's unbalanced
movement   and this ferocity
of aquatic life.

Up above us   brown cliffs
eroded and chancred
by sea and tremors   the beach
sinister with the sound of
wind   sea   birds and distant gunshots.

Coping with sexual history

It's all a question of possession.

My bedmates,
past & present,
sit inside my head.

They are raw & naked meat.
They have taken off their skins
& have come to stay.

"Listen, you cows,
my head is not a home from home
for the likes of you,
nor ever was it so.
Unseat yourselves!"

But, ever one step ahead,
they have screwed meat-hooks
into the roof of my skull
& have hung their hides on these.

I plead with them:
"I never knew the game
had rules as sinister as these.
Had I known, I doubt if I'd have played."

Up there, it is dry
& the skins – never missing a trick –
are quick
to take on the texture of dead leaves.

They answer me back:
"You have taken our bodies;
now you have our skins to keep.
There is nothing sinister in that."

I sit perfectly motionless,
but – fuck them – those female pelts still sway
brushing one against the other
until I cannot think for the noise they make.

Three Gargoyles

I
The wart's inherited the face,
Put a last kiss
On 1880 lips.

Turned to the street,
Both face and wart
Announce their part.

Eternal woman of Canterbury,
Joan Durbeyfield's sister,
Juliet's nurse,
Bloodstream and chorus.

II
Skin smooth as stone
Stretched on this sun-lamped, foam-backed skull,
He'll never trade his tinny trader's soul
For feel of weather.

No sight for little children,
Don't let the squeamish stare.
That body is an artefact,
There is no person there.

III
Grinning, teeth in the wind,
Scrambling higher
To the east face.
Glad of bird droppings,
Any chance thing.
By good fortune silent.
A voice to splinter the stars.

Terra incognita

It must be there, or else the globe
would topple over; there must be symmetry
in sea and earth. The southern breeze
must have a womb to bear it, the albatross
a royal nest. Look for a lobe
that listens to their whimper in imagery
of serpents, populate the seas
with mermaids and fill in the land with dross.

Yes it is there, and men whose lives
are ordered for them face suspiciously
an imagery as strange and vast
as anything they dreamt of. So they fill
their plots with distant plants and wives
and think of home a world away and see
their future grow to meet their past,
and try to bend the light waves to their will.

Meanwhile the men who think they know
it squat unknown and mean inside its heart
or chant to it without an echo
and contemplate no future and no past.
The sun sets and the shadows grow
to heaven, where stars stand gorgeously apart.
Nothing below stirs but a gecko,
the southern breeze and nameless things that last.

Fountains: Spain

A solution of brutal
nudes. Acid
to etch arid
valleys in the stiff sky. Ants

are biggest
in the hungriest countries,
the insects most
vivid against

the patient unglazed
ground that lets
everything pass
that can

without love
or compromise of grass
& only one
will win if ever.

They begin
when bird
tongues cease
to sizzle in

the indelicate sun
until the
morning when
the moon melts.

An ornamental walk once perhaps
of birch, rhododendron, bay
& laurel, now a dense copse
I can only stray
at the edge of until winter cuts
it back, less each year.

For the few yards I can I enter
to lay up wood
though the weather gives little more
than a passing thought for winter
& cows still prefer shade to the sun bored
in an empty sky. Flies fidget.

constantly round sunburnt leaves.
I take the few logs spared
by the seasons, regretting those
that crumble underfoot with the mild
fever smell of fine leaf mould,
undisturbed for years,

that fills the copse.
I salvage what I can
& what I cannot isn't lost.
Remote from human impatience of the seasons
huge logs running with spiders & lice
dissolve back into earth.

Eheu Fugaces

The years, dear Postlethwaite, fly away,
That thinkful wishing
And even your famous virtue cannot stay,
For here comes Old Reaper, swishing.

The years have no taste! No eucharist cup,
No sacrificial fatling
Can make them loiter to savour, to sup . . .
And look! Here comes Old Knobbly, rattling.

The years have no niceness, just long shanks!
There's no overawing
Them with your jawing of your ranks.
(Look! Quick! Who's that blind rat gnawing?)

The way those buggers plod, though, years!
Not fast, but unflagging,
Blind, handless, heartless, thoughtless, without ears,
And bringing up the rear, Old He's-Dead, nagging.

They've no refinement, just guts,
Guts on legs, hobbling,
Jogging along at a speed of knots
Along of Old Swallow, gobbling.

It wouldn't be so bad if the years were lazy,
But, breezily chattering,
They come whooping: Boomps-a-daisy,
Followed by Old Incoherent, nattering.

Postlethwaite, old boy, here's Old Hollows!
He's come. Your shabby
Heirs have tipped the years he follows
As you used to tip the cabby.

Let's try to forget old Postlethwaite, pet!
The years have their teeth in his ample bottom;
He owes the bastards some ghastly debt
And Old Snatch, the bum-bailiff's got him.

But us! Come on, stroke my hair!
Tell me it's not grey but, by firelight, yellow,
Kiss me! There! D'you think Old Rot would dare
Come pestering such a fine fellow?

Oh my darling! Your breast
As you turn, your leg as you peel your stocking,
Your grace as you shed your vest . . .
Dear Christ! Who's that knocking?

Honda 175

Dry-eyed, fist in a sling, his glossy hobby-horse
Battle-scarred and blooded in its first
Encounter with a stony world: I grieved for this,

Remembering all his pride as he roared off,
Reckless and unassailable; grieve for his generation
Which shrugs away the pain I more resent.

I have no love for the machine, but would have wept
And cursed had I been him. These neo-Stoics
Frighten me. Their joys and hates dispose

As easily as tissue. What became of the boy
Who saw his kitten laid out on a spade
Ready for burial after the butcher's van

Had bundled it like offal to the gutter?
You gazed at it in stricken disbelief,
Gathered your strength upstairs, and shaped a grave,

And wrapped her in a decent rag. White mice
Devoured by marauding cats in the garden shed:
It isn't fair, you cried: it wasn't. Nor was this.

Perhaps each fresh assault should numb the soul
A little more, perhaps it is unnatural
To mourn his blackened hand and buckled wheel.

Living without illusions, he will never
Bruise to the core, and bikes can be repaired.
I ransack drawers for his insurance papers.

Sahara

After long years, the event. Coach full of
hope, and indulgent
cynicism.

Struck the new road. How many years
since the old road touched
the old memory?

Where was Kent: the twisting glory,
woods full of purple gloom –
narrow curves and narrow junctions?

Where the towns, villages?
The sudden dark stream of the old
dipping slantwise away?

Sahara! Blind; scent-deaf.
The coach raced on; teams forgotten –
fierce signs said: HERE and THERE.

Kent lost in the long sweep forward.
Nearing the sea, the dark chopped waves
flashing white, only the sea unchanged.

Entering the town, at last, the small road
I knew; old houses still precariously there
– soft with time . . .

but everywhere else; new death –
outside the town, outside the ground –
The Game? Already lost.

The rotted house

Fall of the house of an habitué
Of deep bedsitterland, richly festooned.
A dumb waiter beside Miss Havisham,
Worn chains, useless bell pulls that wouldn't hang
A flea. The dust is riddled here and crawls.

The stains crowding the walls up crooked stairs
Are humped ghosts, knowing as they couldn't be
Alive: milky newspapers in the hall
Leak dead disasters while they cultivate
New ones embodied in rotund woodlice.

The house that Jack built: all fall down: it steals
The various wing-beats, hurtling slates.
Nothing will ever go right here and what's
Already going well could well go off.

Sitting-room

Had he been content here he might have wished
To carry off a corner of the room
In variable lines of memory:
Just how she sat, with flying schoolgirl nerves
Pinned on the chair's edge eager for a shot
At domination of the room despite
The weaknesses he thought perhaps they might
Mutually have signalled over the usual
Proprietary bric-à-brac, the jugs,
The elephants, lined trunk to tail of course,
Nondescript watercolour, arable land
Pallid under a dead accomplished hand
– The similar wide tracts she must have crossed,
Underestimating her perky mind.

Talking

Yes, he risked talking to others:
when light withered in long windows;
through evenings of wine; between laundered sheets.

It solved, to judge by the contortions
their lives entered into, none of their problems:
some gassing themselves, some marrying dolts. Nor his.

And whatever they thought him, he was not.
Nor they what he. At best then, a palliative
rite, as the clasping of gloves extended on sticks.

Pressed closer, a clawed embrace rending.

From Ireland

Green from Ireland,
and a childhood of pushing prams, –
I can imagine your fireship innocence.

You danced all night,
telling them all the ways their lives were wrong;
kept up in London like treading water.

Now, grounded here, you laugh
at yourself then – until you gasp, as if
roots stirred with a sharp pain

for all that laughter is a loosening from:
home; a confirmation gown;
the holy candles of the faithful poor.

Maybe you don't need obols

When I'm found next morning
my teeth in a jar
dead
they'll recite a living
story, what I was
differing with each teller,

I'll hold the truth. 'Grandad
was found next morning
teeth in jar
dead' my friend said.
'Did he look peaceful?' I said
expecting affirmation
'Just very old – he'll
look better
when they put his teeth in
wash prepare him.'

My mother hardly peaceful
in life 'Looked peaceful
the morning they found her'
my father said: he looked
very peaceful,
maybe you don't need obols.

A last walk through Chicago

To Lakeshore, past
The Cubs' Stadium where
cops are planted on
the sidewalk, we,
vessels side by side,
bruising each other, drift –

Finally we reach
the lake. We stare across
a bright lagoon to where
the downtown skyline leaps.
We sit upon the grass,
sipping two frigid Cokes.

Oh love, the silence is
unbreakable. We trace
Our pathway back. Chicago
Threads us with steely rays.

Cyprus of copper
(*a variation on a Maltese theme*)

From outside the ramparts a few sad voices sang –
    'Cyprus of Copper,
    Cyprus whose metal veins
    Muddy the rivers
    And seep through pubic foam,
    Staining the sea with blood,
    However much we desire you
    We shall never possess you by assault –
    Not even if you were El Adin's lamp
    Tongued with an oily wick
    To light the dark night of the mine.'
While from the tower above a voice replied –
    'I am the sentinel.
    I face the other way, awaiting the barque
    That brings the standard of Venice through the base heart
    Of the storm to the harbour below.
    Una Vela! A sail . . . a sail!'

Farewell to Stevie

The last time I saw you was in the stuffy church hall.
Each word you half spoke, half sang,
Dropped like a pebble
Into a quiet pool of silence,
Making a submarine cairn by accretion –
Your poem, your thing.
And the concentric ripples grew wider,
Overlapping each other before dying away.

After the reading you came up to me with a reproachful air.
– Eric, you were asleep!
– Stevie, I protest. I wasn't.
– I could see you at the end of the row. Your eyes were closed.
– The better to listen. I heard every word.
– Your head nodded.
– In time with your A and M chanting.
– Darling, as I looked at you, I couldn't help thinking of
          those oysters.
– Ah! So you've not forgotten?
– What a luncheon party! Norah in that lovely red hat; Cecil
          looking like the Poet Laureate; and you ordering all
          those oysters, which took so long to arrive!
– It was maddening, Stevie, especially as you had such an
          appetite after the investiture.
– They offered no refreshment at the Palace, not even a glass
          of sweet sherry.
– But you got your gold medal.

I still see the quick flick of your smile. But now,
Thinking of the frightened way it went out,
I wonder if you were really smiling at all.
They say that shortly afterwards,
As you lay speechless on your sick bed,
You asked by signs for pencil and book
And firmly ringed a word in one of your poems.
A ripple arrested –
'*Death*'.

Holding Stones

These cottages are wedged with gifted stones;
unshaped corner hulks which are grey through grass
brushing the bulwark of their jutted strength.

It happens, around tea-time, a child will
stub its toe, coming too close from the path,
but the stone will not flinch from its rock-stance.

Too soon, children will learn that endurance
requires a rooted blindness that remains
ignorant of the touch of trivial pain.

The holding stones are still, impregnable.
Generations go by in less time than the
figure passing homeward from gate to door.

Storm water dries insignificantly,
like the scattered drops of labourer's sweat
brushed off before the threshold at evening.

They accept the sun's heat and the snow's bite
but, unaltered by weather, return them
when cloud or warmth break the communion.

Their bulk monitors the wind securely
as a light-house breaks open the sea's rage
against stone and its habitual stand.

Man-withering age smooths them, while wood rots.
The elderly fall within their terms of
reference; they encompass life and death.

Untried by birth, they face outwards; at all
times convinced they will outlast us; only
while building have men moved such holding stones.

Light never was measure, for
us it brought an each, light
swelled a frosted gas-lamp
globe, in such enthusiastic
gaudiness we decided our self-
knowledge, light thrown on the
suborn fact. *Praeterita* :
somewhere a paragraph that
carries to the Alpine chapel,
Ruskin worked at his mountain
climb, ice pick and mineral
strapped across the shoulder.
Now I know strolling through
close trees above Castro Daire
without expectation, and a
boarded chapel where birds
chattered out, and lounging
there the sun turned and
brilliant glass leaded so, an
idle stone could not splinter
one stain suffused from within.
That's the impression allows
our trace after antecedency,
in a language worrying out
content, declared with access
of place, of place for which we
accede, to the cord of time.

Compare the Whooping Cranes

Compare the Whooping Cranes –
    (a dying race)
    which breed in Canada's north-west
    tundra territories,
    prance into the air on rhubarb legs
    and fly
    two thousand five hundred miles
    to the Gulf of Texas,
    to paddle in warm shallow waters
    and shrimpy sandflats –
with that great cartload of cold cinders
the moon,
forever falling
silent
in silent space.

The Minute
Notes for a painting

Delicate and distinct along the shore
They move, engraved like figures on a frieze
Between the distances of sea and sand,
Lapped in the level light: each one distilling
The essence of this minute swiftly slipping
Time's net – left irretrievably behind.

Flexing ecstatic limbs, the mastiff races,
A chestnut streak by the long breakers' curl,
Sun-gilded, with the spindle legs of children
Bare at the water's edge, a single sail
White as a gull.
　　　　　Geranium-bright, that girl
Who gravely leaves grandfather's hand to gather
Shell-treasure, pearl and rainbow, to take home;
Stooping absorbed beside her coloured bucket,
While he, fist clenched at back, remote above her,
Stares seaward, solitary in private dream.

Dog's and child's joy, the ruminance of age –
Unique and mutable substances that fuse
To harmonize in wholeness on the shore:
Lived with a luminous intensity
So rapt and radiant, in the sun's last hour,
As if each celebrating self would prove
Root, core and truth of an identity
Separate, yet single; through its flesh affirm
Simply to be, sufficient clemency.

So in their sculptural design they move,
Patterned on surf, sand, sky and space, secure
In grace of light – imprisoned as in crystal
Which fixes them, imperishably clear:
Poised beyond change and fading – for an instant
Inviolable in the beams of love.

On the remains of a child who died three thousand years ago, found with burial cups beside it

Forceps and hair
Have separated dust from dust to bare
Your spirit's anchor, white
In this sunlight.

Your skull is
A hatched shell, and your hands
Left only channels in the sand
Aeons ago.

Each millennium scuffs
The lessening fact that you were you
A little more. Only the cups
Are good as new.

Who set them down
Beside your silence with delaying
Hands so desperately set upon
New articulations?

Is every palmed oasis,
Graphed zig-zag in the way
Of fate, a climbing-frame for the psyche
From the pale blood of the clay?

The crocks retain
Their full hollow. Whatever belief
Laid them by your drying gaze,
From the gesture springs a grief

That is ours also, a hazard
Of love, a shared extremity that fledges
A marvellous union of all who have leaned
Over hard edges.

'Copernicus, a timid man?'
(*for Eva*)

'Copernicus, a timid man?',
Title of the Polish professor's talk,
His voice a small broken sound,
Broken vessels on his face,
Like Grandfather Crowder's, and the same capacious suit.
His slides stuck in the machine.
Afterwards we sip tea, with milk.
He gave his lectures in the prisoners' camp.
War could not deflect his didactic monologue.
And, Eva, you translate our more pretentious questions.
He struggles in his chair to say goodbye.
Once I collected Polish stamps,
And had an interest in astronomy.
I write into the cosmic void,
A timid man.

Old photograph

The fashion's changed
Since, posing for that unposed photograph,
You looked so hopefully into the camera's eye.
No chemistry of colour then to fix the contrast
Of green taffeta and red hair.
The greyness of the print
Is greyness now of life.
Like scales,
Her talk goes down the stair.

Siege in the sun

We were doing battle
and you, if I remember correctly
had started the whole affair
because
I would not let
your Lord's hunting dogs
sit on
my Lord's geraniums

You never could play fair
and so it was
that we awoke one morning to find
that you
had bribed Baron Sun to burn
with greater intensity that day
to melt our castle walls
carelessly made of butter
BUT
you forgot that your knights
were made of chocolate

So now
I have no castle
and you have no knights

your Lord breeds lapdogs
and my Lord grows tulips.

Embarkation

Recent school leaver
– accumulation of fifteen years' daydream
races homeward
to relate his first day's nightmare.

I can see by the sandwiches
stacked in the perspex container
that we must all lay a head
on a shoulder
sooner or later.

Double Exposure

Transient mascara lash
necessitating countdown on inner-
space shot
– follows
that through our every gesticulation
a thousand spirits speak,
so, to draw a parallel
– head reclined to thigh
in the same instant,
the same thoughts and realisation
of here with paddle in hand
on this last, lone, trans-atlantic
crossing,
or a chess tournament on Blueberry
Hill, head reclined to thigh
– strong odour
of deep generation chasm,
of prehistoric entrails,
of a child in a faded snapshot
smiling
in a wisecrack year.

a country house

the owner's not
been seen for years
(prefers life in town)

but still retains
two gardeners
on weekly terms.

he doesn't pay
until they sue,
so, instead of wages,

they grow beans,
potatoes, on
his twenty acres;

the croquet lawn's
become allotment,
the tennis-court

is poled and strung
for vegetables.
and, to exercise

their gardening skills
they pile the potted
plants around the hall,

train creeper
down the corridors,
and keep the guest-rooms

drenched in flowers.

of course
Giacometti
worked
like that!

have you never
seen your shadow
(walking)
the moon behind
you?

of course
Egyptians
worshipped
cats!

have you never
seen their shadow
(sitting)
the sun behind
them?

no leaves
on
this tree!

when did
the last one
fall?

two leaves
on
this tree!

when will
the last one
fall?

Kathleen Abbott was born in Wolverton, Buckinghamshire, and studied at St Hugh's College, Oxford. She has published two books of poems, *Where the sun began* (1970) and *Masks and Ikons* (1973). She has contributed poems to various periodicals and been broadcast on the BBC.

Ruth Adam was born in Dublin in 1946 and educated there at Trinity College. She has lived in Canada and Paris but has been in London since 1971.

Anna Adams was born in London and educated mainly in art schools. Her publications include *Rainbow Plantation* (Outposts, 1971) and *Parabola* (Headland, 1975).

Fleur Adcock was born in New Zealand in 1934 and studied at Victoria University, Wellington. She works as a librarian in the Foreign and Commonwealth Office. Published collections include: *Tigers* (1967), *High Tide in the Garden* (1971), and *The Scenic Route* (1974), from OUP.

Roger Airey is reading English at Ruskin College, Oxford. Previously he worked as a head gardener in Shoreham. He has been writing verse for fifteen years.

R N Allan was born at Haverton Hill, Teesside. After jobs in industry and teaching he is lecturing in French at a College of Education in Staffordshire.

Graham Allen was born in 1938 in Swansea and was educated at the Universities of Wales and Cambridge. He is now Senior Tutor in English at Coleg Harlech. His poems have been published in *Poetry Wales, The Anglo-Welsh Review* etc. A collection, *Out of the Dark*, has been published by Christopher Davies.

Patrick Anderson has written books of poetry: *A Tent For April, The White Centre, The Colour As Naked* (all published in Canada) and various other books. He edited two magazines in Montreal and was twice awarded prizes by *Poetry*, Chicago.

Geraldine Andrade's poems have been published in *The Lady, Cosmopolitan, Incept* and in 1971 she was a prizewinner in the BBC Woman's Hour Poetry Competition.

R. W. Angus says, 'I'm a schoolmaster/writer, with more time now for some writing'.

Alasdair Aston was born in 1930 at Inverness. ILEA Inspector for English since 1968. Chairman, Dulwich Poetry Group. Member of General Council of the Poetry Society. Awarded Chancellor's Medal 1953, Seatonian Prize 1973 and 1974. Fellow of the Royal Entomological Society; Fellow of the Linnean Society.

Mary Bainbridge was born in Liverpool in 1952. At Wentworth Castle College she began to write poetry. She now teaches in an infant school.

Peter Barry is in his late twenties and now teaches literature. He has been working with the Alembic Poetry Group since 1972, and has published poems in small magazines, including *Alembic 1* and *2*, and *Fix, Kontexts* and

Corridoor. A longer poem, *Breton Days* (Share Publications, March 1975).

Joan Barton was born in Bristol in 1908. For the last twenty-eight years she has been a bookseller. A collection of her poems, *The Mistress,* appeared in 1972. She now lives and works in Salisbury.

William Bealby-Wright studied at the Ruskin School of Drawing and has exhibited in London and Paris. He started writing as a member of the Barrow Poets. Wrote *Moonshine Rock,* a ballad/poem cycle produced at the Hampstead Theatre Club (1973), with music by Jim Parker. They started the group, Doggerel Bank, and made a record based on this piece, Silver Faces (1974).

William Bedford was born in 1943 and worked for several years in the City. He is currently reading English at Sheffield University. He has published poetry and criticism in *Agenda, Ariel, Critical Quarterly* etc.

Christopher Bell was born in 1946 in the East End of London and became a surveyor. He became a community worker in Kensington and Chelsea. Now studying photography full-time and living in Notting Hill.

Robin Bell was born in 1945 and was educated at Universities in Scotland and New York. Now a British civil servant. Two books of poetry published: *The Invisible Mirror* (1965), and *Culdee, Culdee* (1966). Edited the collected poems of James Graham, First Marquis of Montrose, 1970.

Anne Beresford was born in Redhill, Surrey, and studied acting at the Central School of Dramatic Art. She is now teaching drama at the Arts Educational School in the Barbican.

Ruth Bidgood was born in South Wales. She studied English at Oxford and served in the WRNS. Collections of poems are: *The Given Time* (Christopher Davies, Wales) 1972; *Not Without Homage* in June 1975.

Peter Bland was born in Scarborough, Yorkshire in 1934 and emigrated to New Zealand in 1954. He edited the monthly 'Poetry' programme for the NZBC. He has published three volumes of poetry and several plays and poems in the *London Magazine*. He returned to England in 1969 on a Queen Elizabeth II Arts Council Fellowship in Drama.

Martin Booth was born in 1944. *The Crying Embers* (1971), *Coronis* (1973) and *Snath* (1975). He has also written several children's books. He is poetry critic for *Tribune*, runs Sceptre Press and teaches English in Northants.

Keith Bosley was born in 1937 and works for the BBC. *Tales From the Long Lakes* (Finnish legends, 1966), *Russia's Other Poets* (1968), *The Possibility of Angels* (poems, 1969), *And I Dance* (poems for children, 1972), *The Song of Aino* (Finnish ballad, 1973) etc.

Christine Bress was born in 1920 and educated at Kent College. She is a free-lance journalist and broadcaster.

Shirley Bridges was born in 1924; is married with children; lives in Surrey.

Edward Broadbridge was born in 1944 in Leytonstone, London. He trained as a teacher and now lives in Denmark where he teaches English. For the use of Danish colleges, he has edited an anthology of modern English poetry.

Edwin Brock's first collection of poetry was published in 1959. He has published five further collections in this country and two in America. He is widely anthologised, and a selection of his poetry appears in Penguin *Modern Poets No. 8*. He is poetry editor of *Ambit*.

Alan Brownjohn was born in 1931 and is a senior lecturer in English at Battersea College of Education. His collections of poems include *The Railings*

(Digby Press, 1961), *The Lions' Mouths* (Macmillan, 1967), *Brownjohn's Beasts* (Macmillan, 1970), *A Song of Good Life* (Secker and Warburg, 1975).

Ted Burford was born in Hunslet, Leeds, and left school at thirteen. He now works in civil aviation electronics. He won first prize in the 1969 Camden Poetry Competition and is assistant editor of *Limestone* literary magazine.

Jim Burns was born in Preston in 1936. Major collections: *Cells* (Grosseteste Press, 1967); *A Single Flower* (Andium Press, 1972); *Leben in Preston* (Palmenpresse, Germany, 1973). He is a contributor to various anthologies and magazines, including *Ambit, Poetry Review, Tribune, New Statesman* etc.

Richard Burns was born in 1943 in London. Founder and co-ordinator of the Cambridge Poetry Festival 1975. Eric Gregory Award 1972, Keats Poetry Prize 1974. Poetry includes *The Easter Rising 1967* (1969); *Double Flute* (Enitharmon Press 1972); and a considerable number of translations.

Philip Callow was born in Birmingham in 1924. Since 1956 he has published poetry, novels, autobiography and has had plays produced on television and radio. In 1966 and 1970 he was awarded Arts Council writer's bursaries. His published collections of poems are: *Bare Wires, The Real Life* and *Turning Point*.

Jeremy Cartland was born in 1944. His poems have been published in *Poetry Review, Stand* etc.; he has won several poetry prizes. He is a member of a performing group, Salatticum Poets.

Glen Cavaliero was born in 1927. Between 1952 and 1964 he served as a minister in the Church of England. He teaches in Cambridge and has published a book of poems, *The Ancient People* (Carcanet Press 1973).

Ian Caws was born at Bramshott, Hampshire, in 1945 and is a senior social worker with special responsibility for the deaf. He obtained the Eric Gregory Award and was received into the Roman Catholic Church, both in 1973. His first collection, *Looking for Bonfires*, is to be published this year.

Cal Clothier was born in Portsmouth in 1940 and is a Principal Lecturer at Leeds Polytechnic. *Love Time* (Hub Publications, 1973), *Behind Heslington Hall* (York Poetry, 1973), and *Headhunters* (Ryder Press, 1974). In 1971 he won the Guinness International Poetry Prize. He is poetry editor of Orbis.

Jeff Cloves. Poet, songwriter and musician. Lives in St. Albans. Sports fan.

Barry Cole was born in 1936. Four novels and five collections of poems; *Pathetic Fallacies* (Eyre Methuen, 1973), and *Dedications* (Byron Press) being the most recent. From 1970–72 he was Fellow in Literature at the Universities of Durham and Newcastle upon Tyne.

Laurence Collinson was born in Leeds in 1925 and has spent most of his life in Australia. *The Moods of Love* (1957) and *Who is Wheeling Grandma?* (1967), both by Overland Press, and a novel. His plays have been produced widely in Britain, Australia and Canada.

Stanley Cook was born in a South Yorkshire village in 1922 and is now a lecturer at Huddersfield Polytechnic. First in the Hull Arts Centre/BBC Poetry Competition in 1969 and the Cheltenham Festival Poetry Competition in 1972. *Form Photograph* (Phoenix Pamphlet Poets, 1971) and *Signs of Life* (Peterloo Poets, 1972).

William Cooke was born in Stoke-on-Trent and educated at Leeds University. His poetry has appeared in numerous magazines and on BBC. He published a critical biography of Edward Thomas in 1970.

John Cotton was born in London in 1925. *Kilroy Was Here* (Chatto and Windus), was the Poetry Book Society choice for Spring 1975. He edited Priapus, a magazine of poetry and art, between 1962 and 1972, and has been Chairman of The Poetry Society since 1973.

David Craig was born in Aberdeen in 1932. He teaches at the University of Lancaster and is co-editor of *Fireweed Quarterly*. He has written literary criticism (most recent: *The Real Foundations*, 1973).

Peter Dale was born in Addlestone, Surrey, and studied at Oxford. Head of the English Department of Hinchley Wood School, Esher, Surrey, and associate editor of Agenda. *The Storms* (Macmillan, 1968); *Villon* (Macmillan 1973); *The Seasons of Cankam* (Agenda Editions, 1975).

David Day was born in South Lincolnshire in 1932. He was educated at University College, Durham. His verse has been broadcast and has appeared in the *Critical Quarterly, Poetry Nation, Encounter* etc. *Brass Rubbings* is due for publication in Summer 1975.

Peter Dent was born in Forest Gate, London, in 1938 and is a primary school teacher in Surrey. Poetry and criticism published in: *Agenda, Meridian, New Statesman* etc. Represented in PEN *New Poems* 1974. *Proxima Centauri* (Agenda Editions 1972) and *The Time Between: Poems from the Chinese and Others* (Hippopotamus Press 1974).

Donna Dickenson was born in November, 1946, in Connecticut and is now teaching with the Open University. Poems published in *London Magazine, Workshop New Poetry*, and other magazines and read on BBC Radio.

Freda Downie was born in London and was educated in England and Australia. Poems have appeared in the *Poetry Review*, the *Weekend Scotsman* etc., and won the first prize at the Stroud Festival in 1970. *Night Music* (Mandeville Press) is a recent collection.

William Dunlop was born in Southampton and teaches at the University of Washington, Seattle, USA. His poems have been published in most of the leading English periodicals, and in PEN and Guinness anthologies.

John Eddowes has worked in photojournalism and television, and now runs a small printing firm and covers winter sports. He has travelled extensively.

Alistair Elliott was born in 1932 in Liverpool and educated in the US, Edinburgh and at Oxford. He has worked for the English Children's Theatre (Caryl Jenner) and in libraries in this country and in Iran. He has printed a poster of his own poems *Air in the Wrong Place*, 1968, now out of print.

Gavin Ewart was born in 1916 and is now a freelance writer. Verse includes: *Pleasures of the Flesh* (Alan Press), *The Deceptive Grin of the Gravel Porters* (London Magazine Editions), and *Be My Guest!* (Trigram Press).

Padriac Fiacc was born Belfast 1924 and educated in New York City. Returned to Belfast in 1946. Awarded AE Prize for unpublished collection, *Woe to the Boy* (1957). Two other collections, *By the Black Stream* (Dolmen Press, Dublin, 1969) and *Odour of Blood* (Goldsmith Press, Dublin, 1973) were published. Also edited a poetry anthology *The Wearing of the Black*, 1974 (Blackstaff Press, Belfast).

R. A. Foakes was born in 1923, and is now teaching literature at the University of Kent, occasionally publishes poems. He has written two books of criticism: *The Romantic Assertion,* on nineteenth-century poetry, and *Shakespeare: The Dark Comedies to the Last Plays.*

Robin Fulton was born in 1937. *The Spaces Between the Stones* (1971), *The Man with the Surbahar* (1971), *Tree-Lines* (1974). He lives in Scandinavia and has translated several Swedish poets. Also *Contemporary Scottish Poetry : Individuals and Contexts* (1974), and has edited *Lines Review* since 1967.

Roger Garfitt was born in 1944 and studied at Oxford. Guinness International Poetry Prize, 1973; Gregory Award, 1974. First full-length collection, *West of Elm* (Carcanet, 1975). Arts Council Creative Writing Fellow at the University College of North Wales, Bangor, in 1975. Poetry critic of the *London Magazine*.

Peter Gilbert was born in London in 1942 and studied at the Universities of London and Essex. He is a free-lance lecturer in sociology and literature, and is now teaching American students at Grenoble University, France.

Giles Gordon was born in Edinburgh in 1940 and has had poems in the first six *Scottish Poetry Anthologies* (Edinburgh University Press), in *Poetry Dimension 1* (Abacus), and in *Scottish Love Poems* (Canongate). His poems are published in *The Scotsman*. He is a novelist, short story writer and editor.

Henry Graham is a lecturer at Liverpool Polytechnic Faculty of Arts, and poetry editor of *Ambit*. *Soup City Zoo* (Anima Press, 1968); *Good Luck to You Kafka/You'll Need It Boss* (Rapp & Whiting, 1969) and *Passport to Earth* (Andre Deutsch, 1971). He has contributed to national and international anthologies; awarded three Arts Council grants.

F Pratt Green was born in Liverpool in 1903. *This Unlikely Earth* (poems) and *The Skating Parson and Other Poems*. His poetry has appeared in many periodicals and anthologies, including the *Oxford Book of Twentieth Century English Verse*. He is a retired Methodist minister and now lives in Norwich.

Frederick Grubb attended Trinity College, Cambridge. He has published a volume of verse and a critical book, and works in workers' education. Contributor to *Tribune* and Larkin Number of *Phoenix*. Hostile to the professionalisation, commercialisation, and mediaisation of both art and life.

John Gurney was born in 1935 and studied at Oxford. He has received a number of prizes and was awarded a special commendation for a poem at Stroud in 1973.

Michael Hamburger was born in 1924 and published his first book in 1943. University lecturer between 1952 and 1964. *Ownerless Earth* (New & Selected Poems), *A Mug's Game* (Intermittent Memoirs), *Art as Second Nature* (criticism), and *Peter Huchel; Selected Poems* (translation) – published by Carcanet Press.

Christopher Hampton was born in London in 1929. He has taught in Italy and now teaches English at the Polytechnic of Central London. *The Etruscans and the Survival of Etruria* (Gollancz and Doubleday) and *An Exile's Italy* (poems, Thonnesen). Editor of *Poems for Shakespeare 1*, and council member of the National Poetry Centre.

Patrick Hare was born in 1936 and has taught English in Oxford since 1965. Over fifty poems published in *The Listener, Tablet, Encounter, Critical Quarterly* etc. Three English text books (Blackwell & Mott, Oxford) and four unpublished novels.

David Harsent was born in Devonshire in 1942. Senior editor in a London publishing house. He has received a number of literary awards, including the Gregory Award. His most recent book is *After Dark* (Oxford University

Press, 1973); *Truce* (limited edition, Sycamore Press, Oxford, 1973).

J. F. Hendry was born in 1912 in Glasgow. He has lived in Europe and Canada, and now in Scotland. He was co-editor of *White Horseman Anthology* (1942). *Bombed Happiness* (Routledge); *Marimarusa,* a long poem (published in Canada); *The Blackbird of Ospo,* stories (Maclellan).

Cicely Herbert is one of the Barrow Poets and has given readings with the group in the USA, Canada, Germany and Holland, as well as in Britain.

Terence Heywood was born in New Zealand and was educated at Malvern and Oxford. Poems have appeared in many countries, including translations. *Facing North* (Mitre Press, 1960) illustrated with the poet's own photographs, and a number of anthologies. He has won several prizes for poetry.

David Holbrook was born in 1923 in Norwich. He has published four collections of poetry and a novel, besides a large number of books on the teaching of English and the psychology of culture.

Geoffrey Holloway was born in 1918 and educated in Liverpool, Birmingham and Southampton Universities. He is a social worker for Cumbria County Council and lives near Kendal. *To Have Eyes* (Anvil Press, 1972), and *Rhine Jump* (London Magazine Editions, 1974). The latter was a Poetry Book Society Choice.

John Holloway was born in London in 1920; educated locally and at Oxford. Taught at Oxford and at Aberdeen, abroad and Cambridge where he is now Professor of Modern English. Five books of verse.

Libby Houston was born in London in 1941 and studied at Oxford. *A Stained Glass Raree Show* and *Plain Clothes* (Allison & Busby, 1967 and 1971). She has served on the National Poetry Centre's Advisory Panel of Poets since 1974. BBC scriptwriting for children and free-lance editing. Awarded an Arts Council grant 1972.

Peter Jay was born in 1945. While at Oxford, where he won the Newdigate Prize, he founded the poetry magazine, *New Measure*. He now runs Anvil Press Poetry in Greenwich. Publications include *The Greek Anthology* (1973) and various verse translations.

Peter Thabit Jones was born in Swansea in 1951 and studied at Swansea College of Further Education. His poems have been published in *Poetry Wales* and the *Anglo-Welsh Review. Tacky Brow* (*Outposts,* 1974).

Jenny Joseph was born in 1932 in Birmingham. English scholar at Oxford. *The Unlooked-for Season* (Scorpion Press, 1960), *Rose in the Afternoon* (Dent 1975).

Dennis Keene was born in London in 1934. Poems were published in the *London Magazine, Departure* and *New Departures,* and he edited *Oxford Poetry*. Professor of English at Japan Women's University in Tokyo and has a doctorate in Modern Japanese Literature. Translations published by the University of Tokyo in 1974.

Andrew Karpati Kennedy was born 1931 in Hungary and settled in Britain after the war. He studied at Bristol, and is now teaching English Literature at the University of Bergen. His published work includes a recent book on dramatic language, *Six Dramatists in Search of a Language*.

James Kirkup held the Yorkshire Arts Association Fellowship in Creative Writing, Sheffield University, 1974–75. His publications include: *Heaven, Hell and Hara-Kiri, Selected Poems of Takagi Kyozo, Zen Gardens*.

B. C. Leale was born in Ashford, Middlesex, in 1930 and educated in Southend. His poems have been published in most of the leading periodicals in the UK and in anthologies. In February 1975 a selection of his early work, *Under a Glass Sky,* was published by Caligula Books.

Robin Lee held a lectureship in English at the University of Sussex, received a Gregory Award for Poetry in 1972 and wrote the libretto of a children's opera for the Australian composer, Anne Boyd. He died in April 1975.

Laurence Lerner was born in South Africa and now teaches at the University of Sussex. Books of poetry: *Domestic Interior* (1959), *The Directions of Memory* (1964), *Selves* (1969) and *A.R.T.H.U.R.* (1974) as well as novels and literary criticism.

Dinah Livingstone was born in Tokyo in 1940. She came to London in 1966. *Beginning* (1967), *Tohu Bohu* (1968), *Maranatha* (1969), *Holy City of London* (1970) and *Ultrasound* (1974); available from Katabasis, 10 St Martins Close, NW1.

Michael Longley was born in 1939 in Belfast and studied at Trinity College, Dublin. Assistant Director, Arts Council of Northern Ireland. *No Continuing City: Poems 1963–68* (Macmillan, 1969); *An Exploded View: Poems 1968–72* (Gollancz 1973).

Edward Lucie-Smith was born in 1933 in Kingston, Jamaica. *A Tropical Childhood, Confessions and Histories, Towards Silence* and *The Well-Wishers* (all OUP). Edited a number of anthologies, among them *British Poetry since 1945* (Penguin).

Mziri Macinnes was born in 1925 in County Durham, educated in Yorkshire and at Oxford. She has lived abroad and is now in Leeds.

Diana Mcloghlen has written poetry from an early age. Her poem *October Harbour* is one of those representing Ireland in a modern Polish anthology about the sea. *The Last Headlands* (Chatto & Windus) appeared in 1972.

George Macbeth was born in Scotland and now lives in London. He is a member of the BBC's Talks and Documentaries Department. Since 1954 he has published thirteen books of his poetry, including *A Form of Words* (1954), *The Broken Places* (1963), *Collected Poems* (1958–70 and 1971), *In The Hours Waiting for the Flood to Come* (1975).

H. B. Mallalieu published poems in the thirties and during the Second World War. He began writing again in 1970. *Portrait* appeared first in *Poetry* (USA).

Jim Mangnall was born in Liverpool in 1930. His work has appeared in *Ambit, Phoenix* and in various anthologies including the *PEN Anthology 1972. Soup City Zoo* (Anima Press), *Journey to the Middle Earth* (Subvers Press, Holland) and *The Lionheart Letters* (Driftwood Publications).

Alan Marshfield was born in 1933 and is Head of English in a Mill Hill Comprehensive School. *Mistress* (Anvil), and *Dragonfly* (Oasis). He has contributed to Peter Jay's *Greek Anthology* and B. S. Johnson's *All Bull,* broadcast poetry and published in numerous periodicals.

Harold Massingham was born in 1932, at Mexborough, South Yorkshire, and educated at Manchester University. *Black Bull Guarding Apples* (Longmans, 1965), *The Magician* (Phoenix Pamphlet Poets, 1969) and *Frost-Gods* (Macmillan, 1971). He won the Cholmondeley Poetry Award, 1968.

Gerda Mayer was born in 1927 in Carlsbad, Czechoslovakia, and came to

England in 1939. She was educated at Bedford College, London. A selection of her poems will be published by Chatto & Windus in *Treble Poets 2*.

Nigel Mellor was born on Tyneside in 1946 and is a teacher in North Shields. He has been writing poetry for ten years, not previously offered any for publication. The great, great grandson of Joseph Hunter, the poet of Tyneside who, he believes, with some evidence, is the real author of the *Blaydon Races*.

Bill Mercer is 46, and was educated at Hastings and St Catherine's, Cambridge. He teaches English in a state school. He is obsessed with the exact nature of Shakespeare, and dislikes most motor vehicles and television.

David Miller was born in 1950. *The Caryatids* (Enitharmon Press, London) and *All My Life* (Joe di Maggio Press, London), both 1975. Since 1966; clerk, bookseller, library assistant. He has lived in London since 1972.

Elma Mitchell was born in 1919 in Airdrie, Lanarkshire, and studied at Oxford. Now lives in Somerset. Poems in periodicals including *New States-man, Outposts, Phoenix,* and *The Times Literary Supplement*.

Edwin Morgan was born in Glasgow in 1920. Reader in English at Glasgow University. *The Second Life* (1968), *Penguin Modern Poets 15*, with Alan Bold and Edward Braithwaite, (1969), *WI The Haill Voice* (translations from Mayakovsky) (1972), *Instamatic Poems* (1972) and *Essays* (1974).

Pete Morgan lives and works in Yorkshire. His poems were included in *Poetry Introduction 2*, (Faber 1972) and, more recently, in *The Grey Mare Being the Better Steed* (Secker & Warburg).

H. O. Nazareth is an immigrant from Bombay and has been resident in London since 1965. He has completed two (unpublished) collections of poems: *Bannerjee* (Impressions of an Outsider) and *Word-Guerilla*, from which 'This is me on a Bus' is taken. He is a member of the Collective which publishes the magazine *Race Today*.

Hubert Nicholson was born in Hull and now lives in Epsom. He was for many years a journalist with Reuter. *Date, New Spring Song* and *The Mirage in the South*, and twelve novels (the latest, *Ella*, in 1973), as well as essays and memoirs. He is represented in various anthologies.

Leslie Norris was born in 1921 in Merthyr Tydfil, Glamorgan, and studied at the University of Southampton. Six books of verse, the first in 1941. He received the Poetry Society's Alice Hunt Bartlett Prize for *Ransoms* (Chatto & Windus, 1970) and a Welsh Arts Council award for *Mountains Polecats Pheasants* (Chatto & Windus, 1974).

Nicholas H. Nuttall was born in London in 1946. He has worked for two years in East Africa as a quantity surveyor. He has published some short stories. He directs plays with local drama groups.

Robert Nye was born in 1939 in London and now lives in Edinburgh. *Juvenilia 1* (1961), *Juvenilia 2* (1963), and *Darker Ends* (1969). A novel, *Doubtfire* (1967), a book of short stories, children's books and critical reviews for various journals. Poetry editor of *The Scotsman* and poetry critic of *The Times*.

H. J. L. Osbourn is a 54-year-old director of public companies dealing mostly in finance. He has written on company finance and related subjects for the *Investor's Chronicle*, the *Bankers Magazine* etc., and is a regular contributor to *The Times, Country Life*, the *Field*, and numerous periodicals on shooting, fishing and other country matters.

Ewald Osers was born in Prague in 1917; worked for the BBC since 1939. Translated about fifty books including six volumes of poetry. Poems translated from German, Czech, Russian, Serbo-Croat published widely and read on radio and television. His own poetry has been published in a few literary magazines. Awarded the Schlegel-Tieck Translation Prize in 1971.

Valerie Owen was born on London's Essex fringe. She studied at the University of London. She has worked in factories, taught in schools and art colleges. She has broadcast poems on BBC's 'Poetry Now' and contributed to PEN's *New Poems 1973–1974*.

Philip Pacey was born in Yorkshire in 1946 and studied at Cambridge. He is now art librarian at Preston Polytechnic. His poems and criticism have been published in a variety of magazines and anthologies. He has won the Pernod National Young Poets' Competition and received a Gregory Award.

Glynne Painter was born in Worcester and has lived in Scotland, Kenya, New Zealand etc. Now settled in London. Contributor to *Samphire, Envoi* and divers American children's magazines.

David Palmer was born in Portsmouth in 1935 and was educated at Lincoln College and London University. He has recently been appointed head of the sixth form in a large Portsmouth comprehensive school. Poems in *Anglo-Welsh Review, Phoenix, Poetry Wales* and other magazines and on BBC.

Christopher Pilling was born in 1936 and is now Head of Modern Languages at Knottingley High School. In 1970 he won the first new poets award with *Snakes & Girls*. Arts Council grant in 1971 and two pamphlets published. *Bird Poems* to be printed by the Janus Press (Ilkley). Poems in the *New Statesman*, the *TLS*, *Encounter* etc., and on BBC.

Sarah Pope is a viola player who has just left the New Zealand Broadcasting Orchestra to play in the BBC Welsh Orchestra in Cardiff.

Tully Potter was born in Scotland in 1942, but lived in South Africa from 1948 to 1966 and was greatly affected by what he experienced there. He now lives in Essex, where he runs the Poetry One workshop group and little press. He is a journalist on a national newspaper.

Omar S. Pound studied at McGill University and at the Universities of London and Tehran. He has travelled extensively throughout the Muslim world. Teaches at the Cambridgeshire College of Arts and Technology. *Arabic and Persian Poems,* Fulcrum Press (1970), *New Directions,* NYC (1970). *Kano,* Migrant Press (1971).

Neil Powell was born in London in 1948. He has contributed to numerous journals, including *Critical Quarterly, Encounter* etc. He won a Gregory Award in 1969. He publishes poetry and literary criticism. He is the author of the *Henry V* book-plus-tape unit in the 'Studytapes' series.

John Pudney was born in 1909 and since 1942 his publications include poetry, novels, short stories, official documentaries, children's stories etc., as well as a variety of articles in the national press and in journals. Of his nine published volumes of poetry, the most recent is *Selected Poems* (1967–73), Dent. He has just published a social history, *London Docks* (1975, Thames and Hudson).

Rodney Pybus was born in 1938 in Newcastle-upon-Tyne. He took a degree at Cambridge and now works in television in Newcastle. *In Memorian Milena*

(Chatto/Hogarth 1973), was awarded the Alice Hunt Bartlett Prize by the
Poetry Society.

Peter Redgrove has published poetry, plays and novels, and has just returned to England after holding the O'Connor Chair of Literature at Colgate University, New York. In 1975, *Sons of my Skin : Selected Poems* (Routledge). His first novel, *In the Country of my Skin* (Routledge), won the 1973 Guardian Prize. (Geoffrey Glass – see text – is hero of *The Glass Cottage*, Peter Redgrove's third novel to be published in 1976).

Maxine Redmayne was born in 1941 and educated in England and France. She lives in London but only recently had an opportunity to enrol in an ILEA adult education course on writing poetry and prose.

Dennis Reid was born in 1948 in County Antrim but spent most of his life in and around Belfast. He has engaged in a series of 'miscellaneous and arbitrary occupations' and is now reading literature at the University of Essex.

Ian Robertson was born in Sutton Coldfield, near Birmingham, in 1958 and spent most of his life in Cardiff. He has worked in a public library and his interests are literature, philosophy, drama and jazz. He would like to go to Paris 'to seek out Sam Beckett'.

B. D. Rogers was born in Bancyfelin, Carmarthenshire and was educated locally and at University College, Oxford. He was on the staff of *The Times* and the *Daily Telegraph Magazine*. Now living in London, N1.

Harriet Rose is currently working at the Cockpit Theatre in London where she conducts a poetry workshop. She has danced her poems in public performance at the Oval House, London. Her poems have been published in many magazines here and abroad, and she edits *Wheels*.

Dave Rowley was born in 1946 at Newcastle-under-Lyme. Took a teaching certificate in English and Drama. His work has appeared in *Critical Quarterly, Delta* and *Oasis,* and in publications by Plan B of Stone, Staffs.

Lawrence Sail was born in London in 1942, read French and German at Oxford. He has travelled extensively and worked for four years as a teacher in Kenya. He now lives in West Somerset and writes full-time. *Opposite Views* (J. M. Dent, 1974).

Andrew Salkey is a Jamaican poet, novelist, children's writer and broadcaster. He has lived in England since 1952. *Jamaica* (long poem) and *Come Home, Malcolm Heartland* (Novel). He has edited many anthologies of Caribbean writing.

Vernon Scannell was born in 1922. For his poetry he has received the Heinemann Award for Literature (1960) and the Cholmondeley Award in 1974. *Selected Poems, The Winter Man,* and *The Apple Raid* (poems for children). *Not Without Glory,* a critical study of poetry, Autumn 1975.

Peter Scupham was born in 1933, lives in Hertfordshire where he teaches and publishes new poetry from the Mandeville Press. *The Snowing Globe* (Peterloo Poets), *The Gift* (Keepsake Press) and *Prehistories* (OUP).

Mary Seaton was born and lives now on a farm in Aberdeenshire, was educated at the University of Aberdeen and the Guildhall School of Music and Drama.

Stanley J. Sharpless was born in Ilford, Essex, in 1910. His first verse was published in the long-defunct *Everyman* magazine in 1932. Winner of *New*

Statesman Literary Competitions on and off over the last thirty-five years. His verse has been broadcast by the BBC and anthologised in *The Fireside Book of Humorous Poetry, Erotic Poetry,* and other publications.

J. Sharratt was born in Leeds in 1926 and has lived there ever since. He was educated at local council schools and technical college, and worked in various government departments; now in Post Office. He has written verse since he was eighteen.

Penelope Shuttle was born in 1947 and has been publishing poems in magazines since she was fourteen. *An Excusable Vengeance* (Calder & Boyars, 1967), *All the Usual Hours of Sleeping* (Calder & Boyars, 1971) and *The Hermaphrodite Album : Poems with Peter Redgrove* (q.v.) (Fuller D'Arch Smith, 1973).

Jon Silkin was born in London in 1930 and now lives in Newcastle-upon-Tyne where he edits the magazine *Stand*. In 1958 he was awarded the Gregory Fellowship at Leeds University. He has published twelve volumes of poetry including *The Peaceable Kingdom* (Chatto, 1954), *Nature With Man* (Chatto, 1965) which was awarded the Geoffrey Faber Memorial Prize in 1966, and *Poets of the First World War* (OUP, 1972), criticism.

Valerie Sinason aged 28, edits *Gallery,* an illustrated poetry magazine. Poems and articles published in *Tribune, Nova* and other journals. She has taken part in readings/productions at the Little Theatre, Cockpit Theatre etc.

Alex Smith was born in 1944 and has lived all his life in the area of Romford, Essex. He has always worked in the City; currently in a merchant bank. English literature has been his main interest since he was seventeen.

Sydney Goodsir Smith was born in Wellington, New Zealand in 1915. He travelled in France, Germany and Italy. From 1941, he has published fourteen books of poetry including one verse play, *The Wallace* (1960), and *Collected Poems* (1970). He has edited numerous works on Scottish poets and poetry. He died in 1975.

Jon Stallworthy was born in 1935. At Magdalen College, Oxford, he won the Newdigate Prize for poetry in 1958. Since 1961, collections of poetry include *Root and Branch* (1969), and *The Apple Barrel* (1974), a selection from two earlier volumes, now out of print. He has also written two books of criticism, translated poems by Alexander Blok and received the Duff Cooper Memorial Prize in 1974 for his biography, *Wilfred Owen*.

Anne Stevenson was born in Cambridge in 1933, and was educated in the United States. She holds the Compton Fellowship in Creative Writing at the University of Dundee and in 1973 was awarded a Scottish Arts Council Bursary. Four collections of poems including *Living in America* (1965), *Travelling Behind Glass* (1974), and a book of criticism.

George Szirtes was born in 1948 in Budapest and escaped to England with his family in 1956. He studied at Leeds College of Art and has travelled in Italy; he has exhibited in Bradford and London. Poetry has appeared in magazines, including *Ambit* and *The Times Literary Supplement,* and a collection (Perkins).

D. M. Thomas was born in 1935 in Redruth, Cornwall. He read English at New College, Oxford, and now lectures at Hereford College of Education. *Modern Poets 11* (with Peter Redgrove and D. M. Black: Penguin), *Two Voices and Logan Stone*. A new collection *Love and Other Deaths* (Paul Elek) is due to be published.

Anthony Thwaite was born in 1930. He has taught English at the Universities of Tokyo, Libya and Kuwait, worked for some years as a BBC radio producer, and was literary editor of *The Listener* (1962–65) and of the *New Statesman* (1968–72). Co-editor of *Encounter*. Published five books of poems (most recently *New Confessions,* Oxford University Press, 1974) and a selection in the Penguin Modern Poets series.

David Tipton has published poetry, translations and articles in many magazines, including *Poetry Review, Ambit, Stand* and *London Magazine*. *Peru the New Poetry* (LM Editions, 1970) and *Millstone Grit* (Second Aeon, 1972). He has been writing full-time since last year.

Nick Toczek was born in Shipley, Yorkshire, in 1950 and studied industrial metallurgy at Birmingham University. Editor of the *Little Word Machine* and director of the School of Living Poetry. His poems have appeared in a wide variety of publications. *Malignant Humour* (Aquila), *Autobiography of a Friend* (Aquila), both in 1975. The poem selected is from *Stray Bulletins, Letters and Several Urgent Messages,* a forthcoming collection of poetry and prose.

Shirley Toulson, formerly editor of *Child Education,* is now working as a writer and free-lance journalist. Her poems and short stories have appeared in various literary journals, her most recent collection being *The Fault, Dear Brutus* (Keepsake Press).

David Tribe was born in Sydney, Australia, in 1931, spent many years in London as author, poet, broadcaster and journalist, and has now returned to Sydney. Book of poems *Why are we Here?* and individual poems have appeared in *Inter Alia, Tribune, New Statesman* etc. Numerous prose works.

Ben Vincent is a retired civil servant and former schoolmaster. A frequent contributor to Quaker journals, he is the author of a handbook for the staff of children's homes called *Begone Dull Care.*

Eddie Wainwright has worked as a schoolmaster and College of Education lecturer. At present Head of English at Redland College, Bristol. *Lying in Wait* (ed. Harry Chambers, Phoenix Pamphlet Poets, 1971).

Donald Ward was born in 1909 at Belmont, Surrey, and spent his entire working life in the Post Office. He has written poetry since 1955 and published in numerous journals. First volume *The Dead Snake* (Allison and Busby, 1971). This won an award from the Arts Council of Great Britain. *A Few Rooks Circling Trees* (Mandeville Press), will be published in Summer 1975.

Val Warner was born at Harrow in 1946 and educated locally and at Oxford. She has worked as a teacher, librarian and copy-editor. *Under the Penthouse* (1973), a collection of poems, and *The Centenary Corbière* (1974), translations from Tristan Corbière, both from Carcanet.

Andrew Waterman was born in 1940 in London and went to University in his mid-twenties. Since 1968 he has been a lecturer in the English Department at the New University of Ulster: during this period has written and published poetry which has appeared in the usual periodicals and been broadcast. His first collection, *Living Room* (Marvell Press, 1974) was a Poetry Book Society choice.

Isa Weidman says she is an 'aging, slow-maturing wife of dedicated painter, and mother, developing interest in poetry since two sons pursued careers, about eight years ago'.

Daniel Weissbort was born in 1935 and studied at the Universities of Cambridge and London. In 1965 he and Ted Hughes founded the quarterly magazine *Modern Poetry in Translation*. Collection of poems *In An Emergency* (Carcanet 1972), and poetry and prose translations. Visiting Professor in Comparative Literature at the University of Iowa.

Eric W. White was born in Bristol in 1905. Assistant Secretary (from 1945) and as Literature Director (from 1966) of the Arts Council of Great Britain until 1971. *A Tarot Deal and Other Poems* (Scorpion Press, 1962). *Beginnings* is to be published soon.

Ivan White was born in 1929 in Seven Kings, Essex. He studied English at the University of York and has published *Crow's Fall* (Cape Goliard Press, 1969) in London and (Richard Grossman) in America. Poetry has appeared in the *Aylesford Review, Tribune, Envoi* etc. and heard on BBC. He is at present tutor-organiser for the WEA in North Lancashire and in co-operation with Cumbria Poetry Centre.

John Wilkinson was born in 1953. He was Chancellor's Medallist at Cambridge. His work appears in *Grosseteste Review, Great Works* etc.

Kemble Williams lives in Suffolk and was educated at Bristol Grammar School. An ophthalmic optician, he has been co-editor of *Samphire* poetry magazine since 1968 and contributed to many poetry magazines including *Poetry Review, Poetry Workshop* etc., and *Tribune*. Pamphlets: *The Kind Woman* (1967): *Uses of Culture* (1972).

Margaret Willy has published two volumes of verse, *The Invisible Sun* and *Every Star a Tongue*, and various other books (mainly literary criticism); and many poems. She edits the journal *English*, and lectures for the British Council etc. Fellow of the Royal Society of Literature.

Jane Wilson was born in Hampshire in 1923. She trained at Streatham Froebel College and is currently teaching speech and drama at Huddersfield Training College. Contributor to the PEN anthology 1974 and the forthcoming 1975 edition. Poetry pamphlet *Hooligan Canute* (1974).

Stephen Wilson was born in 1941 and educated at Cambridge. He is a social historian teaching at the University of East Anglia.

Susan E. Worth was born in Dorchester, Dorset, in 1951. Her childhood was spent in the village of Stratton and she attended Dorchester Secondary Modern School. She has been a student nurse and is now married with one daughter.

Dave Wright was born in Bridlington in 1945. He left school at fifteen and did various jobs in the North of England. He works with the Yorkshire Electricity Board as a labourer 'enjoying the marvellous north east outdoors'.

Roger Zair was born in Devon in 1947 and now lives in Didcot. A chartered accountant, his favourite poets are Joni Mitchell and Bob Dylan.

Nicholas Zurbrugg was born in London in 1947 and studied at the Universities of Neuchâtel and of East Anglia. He is currently at Oxford, writing his thesis. Contributed to various international reviews and from 1969 has edited and published *Stereo Headphones*, a magazine of experimental poetry.